# DISTANT FIRES

## by Scott Anderson

**with illustrations by Les C. Kouba**

Pfeifer-Hamilton

Pfeifer-Hamilton Publishers
210 West Michigan
Duluth MN 55802-1908  218-727-0500

**DISTANT FIRES**

Printed in the United States of America by Versa Press Inc
10 9 8 7 6 5

Book design by Joy Morgan Dey
Illustrations by Les C. Kouba
Library of Congress Cataloging in Publication Data
90-61838

ISBN 0-938586-33-5

*To my mother and my father.*
*And to my friend,*
*Stephen Egan Baker*

# Acknowledgments

I began writing this book during finals week the fall quarter of my senior year at college. The other day I came upon that original draft and was shocked by how much the text has changed since then. Part of the change has come about because the first attempt was not done out of some sort of burning inspiration to tell the story but out of a desperate desire to avoid studying for my thermodynamics exam. But mostly, I realized, the change is the result of the efforts of people who could see the book not as it was but as it could be and who were able to persuade me to see it through to a different end. I am indebted to all of them.

It was my father who first put a canoe paddle in my hand and my mother who found it hardest to watch me leave my home on that stormy May morning. To my family I owe my love of the outdoors and of life. That love, I hope, has become a part of this book. For this I am deeply grateful and can only offer my apology for making them and Steve's parents suffer far more worry than any parent should have to endure.

Les Kouba brought this book to life. His illustrations capture for the eye what I have tried to describe for the imagination, and his contribution to me and this book cannot be exaggerated.

Finally, I thank the people with whom I journeyed and about whom this book is written. I am grateful to the people of Duluth for watching over us and to the people along the North Shore of Lake Superior for taking us in when we were cold and hungry. I thank the Canadians along the Winnipeg River for sharing their lives with us and the people at Norway House for taking us into their community and showing us what it means to live in the North.

Mike and Kub I thank for letting us follow our course but reminding us of the beauty and joy that was always around us, even on the difficult days in the swamps.

As for Steve, I know that without his skills we wouldn't be able to laugh today about the waves and the wind and the waterfalls. He never once complained, carried the food pack most of the trip and never gave up on me during those hard times when he no doubt wished that he were paddling a solo canoe. He agreed to substantiate the stories I told in this book. And more than anything, for almost two thousand miles of wilderness waters he let me sit in the back of the canoe. There is no greater friend than that, and I have not written about him enough in this book.

Scott Anderson
Duluth, Minnesota

# CONTENTS

# Preface

Storytelling, I am beginning to learn, is a strange and difficult art, particularly when the story involves others.

In writing *Distant Fires* I struggled to capture the full truth. Where I could not—I hid the evidence.

*Distant Fires* is not a story of arrival, but of departure. It is not a story of travel, but of setting out. It is not a book of personal reflections recorded while perched on a rock in the wilderness; instead *Distant Fires* is about crashing into that rock with our canoe.

*Distant Fires* also is an expression of our admiration for people who aren't satisfied just knowing that far-off lands exist. Like those people, my friend Steve Baker and I had to see those lands—and those waters—for ourselves.

So early one spring morning we left our homes in Duluth, carried a canoe down to the shore of Lake Superior and pointed the bow north. Our destination was Hudson Bay.

In 1930 a similar two-person canoe expedition left Minneapolis. In the canoe were two young men—Walter Port and Eric Sevareid. On our trip, in 1987, Steve and I saw many of the places that those two young men had seen. Some things had changed in the intervening years. Some things, I hope, never will.

I am thankful for the people who, over the years, have had the vision to set aside wilderness lands—not to be conquered and developed, but enjoyed.

I look forward to continuing in this tradition so that in another 60 years our grandchildren will see the wilderness we have seen.

HUDSON BAY

MANITOBA

■ **YORK FACTORY**

*HAYES RIVER*

*GODS RIVER*

*Lone Brook Trout of the Apocalypse*

GODS LAKE

● **NORWAY HOUSE**

ONTARIO

LAKE WINNIPEG

*BERENS*   *RIVER*

*Horror at Fish Camp*

**PINE FALLS**

*WINNIPEG RIVER*   **KENORA**

LAKE OF THE WOODS   RAINY LAKE   **GRAND PORTAGE**

NAMAKAN LAKE   *LAKE SUPERIOR*
*Burned Underwear 10 June*

**GRAND MARAIS**

DULUTH
*Start of Trip*

0   50   100
Miles

MINNESOTA

*The curious world we inhabit is more wonderful than convenient; more beautiful than useful; it is more to be admired and enjoyed than used.*

Henry David Thoreau

# CHAPTER ONE

# Baptism

*There must be a beginning*
*To any great matter . . .*

**Sir Francis Drake**

We did *not* tip over on our first day out.

Shoot, we didn't even *leave* on our first day. We'd been gone five days before we left, and it was on the second day, not the first, that we crashed our foundering canoe onto the rocky Lake Superior shore.

I readily acknowledge that our departure didn't come off exactly as we had planned. For example, we never imagined that we might sink.

According to our carefully laid plans, Steve and I would simply take the canoe and put it in the water. From there we would not stop. We'd see what was beyond that next turn. We'd find out where the next portage led.

Unlike all of our previous trips, this one wouldn't start in the car, with the canoe on top. We'd carry the canoe from our houses in Duluth, Minnesota, all the way down to Lake Superior. From there we'd push north, face trial and tribulation and pass test after test of endurance and finally reach our goal—Hudson Bay of the Arctic Ocean—and attain glory. Then the world would look upon us and say, "They did not fail."

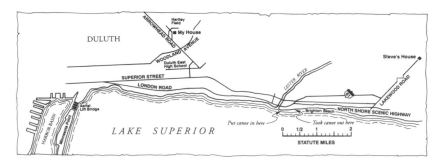

*Scott's and Steve's expedition began on their front steps.*

Unless, of course, we did fail, but we never imagined that either.

It seemed that we'd had to wait forever for the big trip. "Maybe another year," we had heard from our parents. "Maybe another summer."

Later, even we said it a time or two. "I have to work this vacation. Maybe another summer."

In some ways we had been waiting since our dads first took us to the lakes and taught us to carry a pack and paddle a canoe. From those days on we knew we would go. We didn't know where, but we knew we would be ready.

In the summer of my sixteenth year Dad gave me a copy of Eric Sevareid's book *Canoeing with the Cree.* By fall I knew our destination.

In his book Sevareid described how, in 1930, he and his friend Walter Port paddled from their homes in Minneapolis to York Factory on Hudson Bay. They had traveled north via the Red River, Lake Winnipeg and the Gods River, following an old fur-trading route.

Nearly 60 years later, beyond the waters near our homes, lay the same bay, the same ocean. That is where we would go.

When we were 17 we wanted to go, but Dad would permit us to go no farther than Ontario's Quetico Provincial Park, just across the border from the Boundary Waters Canoe Area in Minnesota. Instead of the full summer, Dad allowed three weeks. Then it was college for Steve and me. Maybe another summer.

After our junior years in college we decided we would wait no longer. We were 22, and we knew it was time. We made the plans, earned the money and set the date. The big trip would start in the spring of 1987. We were ready.

By the beginning of May our route was set. During the winter Steve had pored over maps of the north, researching Sevareid's route. With the one hundred Canadian topographic maps we possessed, each laid out with sections of our prescribed course of nearly 2,000 miles, we couldn't miss.

We expected to be gone three months. From Duluth we would paddle up Lake Superior and take the Grand Portage to the border route of lakes and rivers that separate Minnesota and Ontario.

These lakes would carry us along the fur-trading routes of the past and into Lake of the Woods, where we would pick up the Winnipeg River.

Once there we would follow the river into treacherous Lake Winnipeg. A third of the way up the lake we would meet Sevareid's path and pursue it, as he described, over swamps and streams to Gods Lake. Gods River would take us to York Factory and the ocean.

At Norway House, near the top of Lake Winnipeg, we would await the arrival of Steve's brother Mike and our friend, Bill Kubiski. They would be driven in by another of Steve's brothers over a thousand miles of wilderness road to the Norway House settlement. Mike and Bill, in their canoe, would join us for the push to the ocean.

The next order of business was securing a canoe. Given our financial situation, it was not so much a matter of choosing the right canoe as simply getting any canoe. Steve and I both expected to use the aluminum Grumman that we had used since some time right after aluminum had been discovered. We knew that the 80 pounds of the boat would burn into our shoulders on portages, but we had grown up paddling the Grummans. We were used to the pain and were willing to put up with such a boat. Not only that, we already had one.

Still, we made an effort to secure a more suitable canoe. We had written to We-noh-nah Canoe, asking if the people there might have a boat we could use. A Minnesota trip should have a Minnesota canoe, we wrote in our most convincing manner. When the reply came from Winona, Minnesota, I tore open the envelope in anticipation.

On the crisp letterhead I saw the words that made my pulse race. "We have a boat that you can use," it said. Reading on, I saw that we were being offered an eighteen-and-a-half foot Odyssey canoe along with a pair of Maxcraft paddles. The paddles were bent at the shaft and made of composite graphite and Kevlar and weighed just 14 ounces.

The boat had "seen a little bit of use," the letter said, but would be a great canoe for the trip. The Odyssey, with its Kevlar shell and a special PVC foam core for rigidity, was built to handle big waves. And it weighed just 47 pounds. We were glad to take it.

As it turned out, the "little bit of use" the Odyssey had seen had come during the split second it takes for a canoe to hit the pavement after falling off a truck doing 55 down the highway. The back end had broken off and had been repaired with a quarter inch of Fiberglas. "Stronger than new," we were told. Well, at least we didn't have to worry about scratching it.

While in Winona to seal the deal we got our first eerie warning about what lay ahead. Sitting in the office of Mike Cichanowski, We-no-nah's owner, we were pointing out our intentions on maps strewn over his desk.

"I don't know about Lake Superior," he warned. "It isn't a canoe lake. You could get laid up for three weeks without even getting on the water. I'm not sure it can be done. Probably better to start at Grand Portage."

Cichanowski's words, along with our own fear of the big lake, prompted an unconventional addition to our gear. Normally canoes are left open. But, on the advice of Duluth canoeist Jim Wheeler, we decided to build something to try to keep Lakes Superior and Winnipeg out of the canoe—a spray cover. Ours would be different than Jim's, though. He had told us of tipping his canoe over in some northern rapids. Caught upside down in the cover, he had bounced along the bottom, unable to release the zippers. I figured we'd use a different design with Velcro instead of zippers. We wanted our cover to pop open in an emergency.

We had had years of anticipation, but we held to the views of the traditional school of trip planning and thus reserved the bulk of our preparations for that special time when the clock stands still and the expedition really takes shape—the night before.

Purists even avoid the use of a list (regarded as a novice's crutch) and thrill at the thought of pulling through the hardships of forgotten gear. Both Steve and I had seen the experts at work.

"Oh, don't bother writing that down," one would say, "I'll bring the tent poles from my house in the morning." Of course, it is better to get the other guy to say this. A really good planner will maneuver all night just to be able to get a partner to make such a promise. That way he can enjoy the experience of a week long trip without such items as paddles and not have to take the blame for forgetting them.

Later he'd have his say. "Heck, we spent seven days on the Kawishiwi without paddles. Bob forgot 'em on his porch, so at the landing I went out and cut a couple of poplar poles . . . ."

But Steve and I didn't yet feel qualified to work on this level. So, combining the experiences of years of outdoors living, we worked out a complete list of items necessary for wilderness survival. If we had room, we thought, we would take some of them.

Originally, we wanted to take only a Sven-Saw and maybe a ball of twine. As time progressed, however, we expanded the list. On the day we left, we carried the following equipment:

*Odyssey canoe*
*two Maxcraft paddles, two wooden paddles*
*1 No. 3 and 1 No. 4 Duluth Pack*
*2 lifejackets*
*1 four-person nylon tent*
*2 pairs trail pants*
*1 rain jacket*
*2 wool hats*
*shorts*
*1 small ax*
*1 fillet knife*
*bottle of bug dope (didn't help)*
*100 feet of small nylon rope*
*4 fishing rods, 3 reels and tackle*
*300 dollars cash*
*50 1:50,000 scale maps*
*2 compasses*
*2 bottles of fuel*
*sun lotion*

*one spray cover*
*two sponges*
*old rucksack with cook kit and fire grate*
*2 sleeping bags*
*8 pairs wool socks, 2 pairs cotton socks*
*3 wool shirts*
*1 poncho*
*4 T-shirts*
*2 sheath knives*
*1 Sven-Saw*
*1 whetstone*
*matches and lighters*
*50 feet of larger rope*
*first-aid kit*
*2 cameras, slide film*
*10 1:250,000 scale maps*
*1 small cooking stove*
*duct tape*
*harmonica*

For food we left with:

| | |
|---|---|
| 20 pounds macaroni | 10 pounds spaghetti |
| 5 pounds flour | 5 pounds corn meal |
| 5 pounds rice | 10 pounds pancake mix |
| 4 pounds dried potatoes | 2 pounds GRAPE-NUTS |
| 2 pounds oatmeal | 2 pounds Red River Cereal |
| 1 pound dried beans | hot chocolate |
| tea | 2 pounds sugar |
| 1 quart oil (for cooking fish) | powdered cheese |
| instant soup | bouillon |
| spices | pudding mix |
| millet | cooking starch |

We wanted to leave somewhere in the middle of May, just after the opening of Minnesota's fishing season. That way we knew we could get in one last fishing trip before we left. Eventually, we settled on the 18th, which was almost a month before Sevareid and Port had left their homes.

Spring had been mild by Duluth's standards. The snow was gone before April, and the days had been calm and warm. On March 7, Steve and his brother Scott had paddled a mile out onto Lake Superior without seeing a ripple. The sun had been so intense that they had peeled off their shirts to soak up the rays. We should have left that day.

I slept well the night before we were to leave, not so much from the ease and security that comes from proper planning as from the fact that we had been up until three in the morning trying to pack the gear. We had lost the list somewhere in the garage, but Steve promised to bring it and the other gear with him in the morning. Things were looking good.

My mom woke me softly in the morning, whispering that I might as well sleep—we wouldn't be leaving in such high winds.

I, of course, assured her that we were equipped to handle bad weather. But I agreed to drive down to the lake to check on things. On the way, as I swerved down the road trying to avoid the branches strewn about, I began to feel bad about dismissing Mom's assessment so quickly. By the time I reached the water and could see the eight-foot waves, I had decided to hold off a day or so just to make Mom feel better.

That night I bought a new lifejacket. Steve and I decided to leave the next day come "hell or high water." We didn't expect that it would actually come to that.

I carried a canoe and a light pack the four miles from my house to the lake. Steve got to carry the 130-pound food bag and the gear pack over the nine miles from his house. At the half-mile mark Steve decided to jettison the food to his brother's truck. After all, this carry was merely symbolic.

Our departure was carefully chosen to coincide with the time the Broderius kids would be heading off to school. They knew the way to the lake and I didn't want to take any chances. When I got to their house, halfway to the lake, the hardships had begun and I began to feel that the trip was actually happening. The blisters on my heels had come up nicely over the past two miles and had forced me to change to my brand new boots. Later Steve told me that the gas bottles had leaked all over him. It was getting exciting.

Our first destination was Brighton Beach, two miles of smoothly worn gravel, rocks and boulders near Lester River. Brighton Beach is where the the Scenic North Shore Drive begins, and it had seemed the perfect departure spot. Lake Superior had other ideas.

When we arrived, the water was smooth and the air reasonably calm. A slight mist hung over the lake. The sky was a miserable gray, but the crashing waves of the day before were gone. We pushed off.

By the time we rounded the submerged rocks that had been our protection, we realized that Superior had been toying with us. Now, as we left the natural protection of Brighton Beach and as the wind kicked up and the waves began tumbling over the bow, the lake began laughing—laughing at our youth, at our inexperience, at the way we had so confidently outlined our plans to well-wishers only moments before.

Positioned in the stern, I began to feel the water on the bottom of my thighs. Our spray cover, pulled on poorly in a hasty departure, was being stripped away from the sides of the boat by the pounding seas. I knew we would have to pull in. "Pull in," I thought, "after only five minutes on the water?" It would be humiliating.

But, viewing the growing waves and dangerous shoreline from our sinking canoe, I knew pride was the least of our concerns. Our only consolation was that the sound of the crashing waves kept our angry words from the ears of the onlookers gathered on shore.

In the wind the boulders along the scenic beach become terrible fists, jabbing in and out of the waves—now hidden, now seen—threatening to tear a boat apart. But we had to land, and in these waves we would have only one chance.

We really didn't tip. Not exactly. Almost miraculously, we somehow managed to maneuver the canoe through the gaps in the boulders, threading our way unknowingly between certain disasters. In the violent motion of a single wave we were tossed up on shore. The next wave tipped the canoe and filled it with water as we scrambled to drag it up the beach.

Scattered about us were the remains of the breakfast biscuits Steve had thrown in the bottom of the canoe for a morning snack. I looked at Steve and could see in his eyes that he was thinking the same thing I was. We hadn't conquered, we hadn't even escaped—we had been baptized!

# CHAPTER TWO

# The Shore

*"He must have been discouraged", he added.*
*"They go quickly when they are discouraged."*

**Robert Rogers**
from *Northwest Passage*

The first night of the trip was much like the first day.

After dragging the canoe up from Brighton Beach we portaged a couple of miles north to the shoreline home of some friends, the Storsteens.

They are canoeists themselves and didn't want to offend the spirit of our trip, so they offered us a place in the back yard for the tent. It was raining heavily by that time, and we suggested that maybe we should just spend the night in the house. The tent stakes might ruin the wet lawn, we said. The Storsteens insisted that this would not be a problem.

The next day, after draining the water from our tent and clothes, we walked another two miles up the shore. We stopped at the Kirchmaier's Lake Breeze Motel. Mr. Kirchmaier didn't like the idea of our pitching a tent around the cabins, so he made us stay inside the house.

At the Lake Breeze, held captive by the great lake, Steve and I doctored our painful feet, cutting patches for our blisters from the smooth pad of moleskin Mom had slipped into our first-aid kit. We

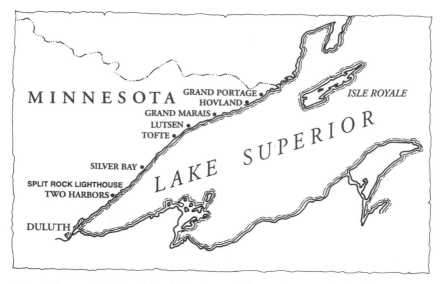

*To residents of the Northland, this beautiful stretch is simply the Shore.*

had assured her that we wouldn't need it but took it anyway just to make her happy. Sometimes you just have to do that for people.

We also developed our modified Gandhian philosophy of passive resistance. We could never match the force of Lake Superior, we knew, but if we could just keep throwing the canoe at it, taking all the punishment it could dish out, maybe it would give just enough to let us by.

With new-found resolve we prepared to wait out the storm.

As the days slipped by during our wait, Steve's dad faithfully kept us informed of the marine forecast. He's a shipping agent and had ready access to the most accurate predictions available. With each report of worsening weather he added the offer to drive us up the Shore to Grand Portage. "After all," he told us, "the whole point is to have fun." But the point was more than that. We couldn't let the lake beat us. Not before we had begun.

On May 23, we got the break we had been waiting for. The skies had cleared and the winds were diminishing. Launching from the steep shore into the still-heavy seas would be difficult, but once we were out in the lake, we thought, we would be all right. We would have to be careful. In the 45-degree waters of Lake Superior a spill far from shore would be deadly.

And then we were on the lake. It felt good finally to be moving. The water was a great pattern of rolling swells, the leftovers of the storm that had so long held us prisoners on land. These swells weren't dangerous, and we quickly learned how to roll with them in our long canoe.

After four days we had finally made it out of the Duluth city limits. Steve calculated that at this rate the trip would take just about 50 years. We hoped to pick up the pace.

The best water was well out from the tumultuous seas of the reflected waves close to shore. We stayed a mile or more from shore where the swells were smooth and coming from just one direction. The only problem was the uneasiness we felt from losing sight of land when we were deep within the troughs.

By the time we reached Two Harbors, 25 miles northeast from Duluth, we were tired but still driven by the memory of the long wait. We would take whatever we could get. We paddled on.

The sun had been gone a good hour when we finally pulled the canoe up just short of the massive cliffs below Split Rock Lighthouse. We were willing to paddle through the night but knew the looming darkness of the cliffs was no place to be in a canoe.

That night was cold. Because we wanted to get an early start the next morning, we simply rolled our bags out on the dewy ground. As we lay shivering we thought about the day. We had seen only one other boat in the 40 miles we had covered. It had been the speedy skiff of the sheriff's rescue squad. Just after Two Harbors the craft had powered its way toward us. "Probably need some help with a tricky rescue operation," Steve surmised. But they had just waved and continued on.

The next morning heralded a beautiful day. We had seen Superior at its worst and now we were seeing it at its best, a shining beauty glittering in the sunlight, cloaked majestically in shoreline green.

After lingering for a moment on the motionless water, we set the canoe in motion. At the base of Gold Rock, just north of the lighthouse, we glided over a silent reminder of the big lake's power. Beneath us lay the wreck of the Madeira, the steel barge that, early in the century, had felt the rage of Superior. On November 28, 1905, in a violent snowstorm the Madeira had broken loose from the steamer William Edenborn. Adrift from its towline, the Madeira was battered against the cliffs. Finally, in two pieces, it sank. Nine of its crew members were saved when seaman Fred Benson jumped from the Edenborn onto the face of the cliff and was able to lower a line to the sinking Madeira.

As we paddled over the Madeira, its hull wasn't visible to us, but we could see the marker-buoy line that dropped to the vessel below. Our eyes followed the thick cable until it disappeared into the darkness. We slipped away.

That afternoon we pushed off from Baptism River, making our way around Shovel Point toward Taconite Harbor, another 20 miles away. This trip was our first taste of big-lake paddling. Both Steve and I were used to canoeing in the Boundary Waters, where the day is broken up repeatedly by the portages that connect the smaller lakes. Always nuisances and sometimes hardships, the carrying places at least serve as markers by which to measure distance.

On Superior, though, distances are immense, and goals are not quickly reached. For five hours during this paddle we stared at the same spot on shore—the tall and rusted docks of Taconite Harbor— trying to fill our minds and take away the boredom. The only occasional reference showing our movement was the odd piece of birch or balsam branch that drifted by.

I sat in the stern. Steve was in the bow. We were trying to make our strokes come together, to work out a rhythm. It was coming slowly, but I guessed that we had time.

Several hours later we passed the Temperance River—so named, it is said, because it's the only river on the Shore that doesn't have a bar. Paddling near the mouth were other canoeists. They were in search of lake trout.

As we approached, one of the men shouted something at us. The press coverage of our departure had overcome our brains, and I guess we expected that the man wanted to wish us luck. Instead, when we drew closer, we heard him yell "you're dragging your shirt in the water!"

Properly humbled, we thanked the man and pulled in the soaking shirt.

As we reached Tofte, we met a man who actually had heard about the trip. "Where was it you left from?" asked the man.

"Duluth," we replied, expecting the man to be impressed. He was.

"Wow," he replied, "that's pretty good for a day." That hurt.

The next day Steve and I again were forced by the wind to take the battle to land. We portaged the 10 miles from Tofte to Lutsen. We had tried to work our way along the shallow bays, but the five-hundred-yard reward for half an hour of work was just not enough.

Once on shore in Tofte we met Bud Tormundsen, the uncle of my old high school band director. After buying us coffee, Bud arranged to have some of our gear (most notably our elephantine food pack) carried to Lutsen in a pickup. Steve and I took to the road, carrying the canoe. At the Lockport Store we picked up the food and accepted the offer of a spot to pitch the tent.

The store was a center of activity for people living along the Shore. The proprietors, Willie and Jo, invited us in for breakfast the next morning. Sitting off quietly to one side, munching happily on cinnamon toast, we took in the people of the Shore.

That's what it is called—simply the Shore. If you've come from Iowa or Arizona you might call it the North Shore. You'd probably buy a postcard at the Beaver Bay sports store and send it back home. "Having a great time here on the North Shore of Lake Superior. Wish you were here."

But if you came from the Northland, say from Lutsen, or Duluth, you'd just call it the Shore. "Let's pack up a lunch and take a drive up the Shore," you'd say.

Steve and I had driven up the Shore a hundred times—or more. But this time it was different. There was no hurry. No car. And a different perspective. We saw what the lake saw.

Everyone we met that morning had a story to tell. All of the stories reflected a similar attitude toward the lake, the Shore and the life. Superior shaped their lives. The lake is not something that can be taken lightly. In spite of its grace it can be a powerful adversary, beautiful and threatening.

In the winter the wind whips through thick Superior ice shards stacked up against the shore. Some say that when the conditions are just right, the ice sings. Deer, engaged in their own thoughts amidst this music, wander far out onto the ice. Sometimes they become confused by open water, panic, and perish.

One of the stories we heard during our stopover was from Lyman Clay, who told us of his escape from the lake steamer America. From 1903 to 1928, before the construction of the modern shoreline highway, the America had carried passengers and freight up and down the Shore from Duluth to Thunder Bay. The lake passage was the only scheduled link between many isolated island communities.

One of those communities was on Isle Royale, and it was there that the America met its end. In the chill predawn hours of June 7, 1928, shortly after leaving Isle Royale's Washington Harbor, the ship struck a rock and began to go down. All 45 aboard were saved, including Clay, only 16 at the time.

That afternoon we split wood and hauled railroad ties in exchange for a new voyageur pack from the small sewing shop a few hundred yards from the Lockport Store. Toward evening the weather improved somewhat, though the fog was still thick, and we pushed off to see if we could make a few miles. At every cabin site we saw people standing on the shore, waving us on. Later we learned that a telephone chain had been formed. Each household called ahead to let the neighbors know about our progress. The smiling faces helped cheer the gloomy air.

Still the fog was a problem for us. To keep from becoming disoriented we were forced to stay within sight of land, and we couldn't cut across the bays. Increased mileage!

After a couple of hours we saw two women standing on high ground, waving us in. "Warm beds! Hot water!" they were shouting. "Come ashore!" That was all we needed to hear. Of course we would miss sleeping in wet sleeping bags on cold rocks somewhere, but we figured that it might be better to sort of gradually get acclimated to this camping thing.

Twenty minutes later we stood with Edna Johnson and her sister, Hazel, within the walls of their huge old house overlooking the lake. The building was worn from generations of use. Carved on a wooden plaque hanging in the kitchen were words that we learned were practiced in that house:

*Guest:*
*You are welcome here;*
*Be at your ease.*
*Go to bed when you are ready.*
*Get up when you please.*
*Happy to share with you,*
*Such as we've got:*
*The leak in the roof,*
*The soup in the pot.*
*You don't have to thank us*
*Or laugh at our jokes.*
*Sit deep and come often;*
*You're one of the folks.*

Edna apologized for the poor quality of the two loaves of excellent fresh baked bread we had inhaled. What a feast!

Before eating we had exchanged our wet clothes for damp ones, stripping off our soggy gear in the basement of the house. All around us were signs of life on the Shore. Three or four pairs of boots stood in the corner, their limp and leaning tops bearing testimony to years of hard use. Scattered on the old roll-away couch were ancient hunting magazines. Several buck racks stood guard over the domain.

We added our sodden shirts to a long rack of wool shirts that had once been hung to dry. Our shirts were new and looked oddly out of place, lacking the holes of the shirts already on the rack, lacking also the smell and the memories that make a truly comfortable shirt. But ours were wet—and that was a start.

The big country house somehow felt empty. A sadness was present in the halls where joyous hunting and fishing parties for generations had gathered. The week before, we learned later, Edna's husband, Gust, had been putting a new coat of paint on the house—trying to make up for the harsh winter and make it ready for the season to come. The ladder he was on had slipped and he had fallen to the ground below, breaking his back. He was recovering in the hospital in Duluth.

"Gust loves the lake," whispered Edna. "He'll be glad that we had you in."

We paddled 10 miles the next day, May 27, our eighth day out.

We encountered more fog and were forced to hug land. After several hours we noticed that the previously moderate wind was picking up. Searching the shore for a landing place, we saw only steep, rocky banks that were being pounded by the-ever increasing waves. The bow of the canoe began riding under the waves, and although the spray cover was secured tightly, we started taking on water. We had to get ashore, but attempting a landing on the cliffs around us would mean certain disaster. So we pressed on, riding lower and lower in the water.

Finally we spotted a small bay with a short gravel beach. If we could make that beach we might get wet, but we wouldn't lose our outfit.

We turned and surged past the solid timber dock of a fish camp. As we hit the beach we jumped out of the canoe and dragged it out of reach of the hungry breakers. A quick survey of the towering cliffs around us revealed an awful truth: We were safe but we were also prisoners.

At times like this emotions run high. It is easy to panic but important to remain calm and determine a plan of action. So we pulled out the gorp, lit our pipes and pointed them thoughtfully at the cliffs that had us penned in. "We're gonna die," I said.

After several minutes of this we decided that since escape by water was impossible we would have to think about scaling the walls. A small waterfall was trickling above our heads. Hoping that it offered a way out, I gave it a try. Steve fished. Twenty minutes later I reached the highway.

In a short time I came upon the home of Clayman Koss, the commercial fisherman whose dock we had passed in our dash for shore. Koss, an enormous man who split his time between working the ore docks at Taconite Harbor and fishing on Lake Superior, had just come off the lake and was measuring and tallying the fish he had taken. The information would be given to the Department of Natural Resources to aid in keeping track of the lake trout populations. Fishermen are allowed only a limited number of lake trout per year. Koss showed me a good number of fish with a missing fin, the mark used by the department to indicate that the fish had been stocked. Over the past 10 years, Koss said, the percentage of native fish in the lake had decreased rapidly.

After we finished sorting the fish, Koss offered to help us land our canoe if we could make it back to his dock. "You'll have to move," he said. "That spot you're on is a state-designated gull breeding ground." Back home in Duluth these nuisance herring gulls are known as "flying rats." Here they had a special territory for breeding. I had to laugh.

I wasn't laughing about getting the canoe off the lake. Even with Koss's help, the trip would be dangerous. But we couldn't carry our gear up the cliff that I had climbed, so the alternative was to sit indefinitely on the section of gravel and wait yet again for the wind to abate.

Landing the canoe on the slippery wooden timber was a tricky operation. The boat was thrown up and down by the waves. Finally, though, the canoe was safe. We had been forced off the lake again, but at least now we could take to the road and move up the Shore. We would hike the nine miles to Grand Marais rather than wait out the wind.

I loaded the center of the canoe on my shoulders. Steve hoisted his burden and grabbed the front of the canoe to steady it against the crosswinds from trucks on the highway. This was painful and awkward, but we figured it would be good practice for the portages to come.

The distance from Koss's house to Grand Marais was just a hop in a car—no farther than an ordinary drive just to go out to eat or to a movie. But with a canoe on your back, walking slowly along the blacktop, distance becomes more significant.

Hanging on an iron post sunk deep into the gravel roadside, in faded paint, a sign called to those needs felt deep within: *Eat, Bowl and Relax.* By the time we saw the sign Steve and I were weary, but we didn't yield to the temptation and traveled on. Someday I will return.

When we arrived at the Grand Marais marina we put into the water and paddled the half mile to the center of town. It was growing late and our first thought was of finding a place to camp for the night.

We pulled the canoe and our gear out of the water and asked some folks about a place to camp. They wouldn't hear of it. A man stepped out of the crowd and offered his hand. "My name's Dean Gulden," he said. "How about staying at our place tonight?"

Before leaving for Dean's house we accepted Roy Steinbrecker's gracious offer of dinner at his Pierre's Pizza restaurant. We ordered the voyageur pizza with everything. It was the name. We were still interested in keeping to the spirit of our trip.

As we quaffed mugs of chocolate milk and dug into the gigantic pizza, we were joined by Holly Nelson. As young boys, Holly and his friends had "run the booms" in the Grand Marais harbor. Logs had been chained together and strung along to enclose lumber floating in the bay. The true test for a young man in those days was to be able to run along the entire distance of the booms without falling into the water, or at least without staying in the water. We bet Holly had been a master.

Before we left the restaurant a man came in and handed us a white paper package. "This is for you," he said and turned and walked away, not waiting for a reply.

"Thanks," we called out, wondering what could be in the package. Steve carefully unwrapped the paper and revealed a bundle of golden hued smoked herring. We were overjoyed.

That night at Gulden's was like a new beginning for the trip. Dean and his wife, Jean Gulden, were themselves preparing for a trip with the kids. Duluth packs were taken from their secret, musty hiding places, and clothes and foodstuffs were arranged, first haphazardly and then neatly into piles.

The Gulden children, Nicole and Eric, were eager to help. As Dean busied himself arranging contents in small canvas gear bags, Eric tried in vain to shoulder one of our heavy packs. Leaning forward in true voyageur style, Eric strained to balance the load on his back. It probably weighed twice as much as he did. He would stagger a few feet forward, then sideways and then fall on his back, struggling like an overturned turtle to right himself.

Early the next morning, standing by the lake to see us off, Dean asked Eric if he thought he could ever take a trip like ours.

Thinking back to his determination with the pack, we knew it was we who could learn from the determination of the boy. With a handshake, we slipped out into the still fog.

Four hours of steady paddling brought us to the village of Hovland. There we pulled up the boat and ate some of our smoked fish. While stretching our legs we came upon Kurt and Ruth Johnson. Kurt had been in the Army during World War II, and Ruth had been one of the first American female Marines.

She still had the boots she had been issued when she joined the Marines. Slightly lifting the hem of her heavy khaki trousers, she showed the boots to us. They were dark brown and deeply polished. The years had robbed them of nothing.

When we pushed out of Hovland we could see that the weather was beginning to clear and the wind was dropping. After several more hours we found ourselves slipping through glassy water. The boulders below, a good 20 feet down, were as clear as if they had been just inches away. The lake was saying, "You see, I'm not so bad." But we knew this was just a disguise. We had seen its real face, and we wanted off.

In our eagerness to make progress we overshot our destination and made land at the wrong side of Hat Point. We had to backtrack. Finally we reached our intended landing point and for the last time touched the nose of the canoe on the shore of the big lake.

Steve and I looked at each other with deep satisfaction. Lake Superior was behind us. Here on land we could use the words we hadn't dared use on the water. We had conquered the lake and it was ours. Here it could not retaliate. Triumphantly, I stepped from the boat, caught my foot and stumbled backwards—splashing one last time into Superior's icy grip.

# CHAPTER THREE

# Grand Portage

*No pain, no gain.*

**Anon.**

The word "miles" should never be applied to a portage.

Whoever thought of measuring the lengths of paths between lakes with "rods" had the right idea. Only an unfortunate few actually know that the rod is sixteen and a half feet. Fortunately I am not among them, and I have trod many portages in a delightful fog of ignorance.

The Grand Portage did not afford us this luxury—nor any others. The ancient carrying place of the voyageurs, the Grand Portage is a nine-mile hike, uphill, and we knew it.

This pathway around the last treacherous miles of the Pigeon River was the final test the voyageurs faced before meeting the big-lake paddlers at the Grand Portage Fort. At the fort, furs were exchanged for supplies and trading goods that were brought from Montreal in the 600-pound *Canot de Matre*. The smaller canoes of the north weighed half that and could more easily handle the rough rapids and difficult portages of the inland waters.

Each spring the two groups of paddlers would depart for Grand Portage. From far in the north, having spent the winter collecting furs from the Indian trappers, the Nor'westers *(hommes du nord)* would set out with their load for the shores of distant Lake Superior.

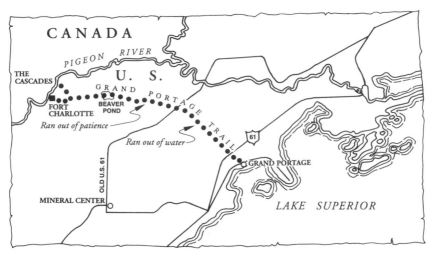

*The Grand Portage—what a lovely name for such a miserable experience.*

From Montreal, the Porkeaters *(mangeurs du lard)* would leave loaded with goods. After the exchange, the canoeists would hurry for home, trying desperately to beat the ice of winter.

The treaty of 1783 between the United States and Britain established that Grand Portage was on American soil. After this the North West Company moved its operations north to Fort William, and the Grand Portage fell out of use. With the merger of the North West Company and the Hudson Bay Company in 1821, followed by the coming of the railroads and other transportation, the old fur-trade route began its rapid decline.

But in its day, the Grand Portage was one of the most important paths in North America. It was this trail that we intended to travel.

Alexander Mackenzie recorded that the voyageurs—often carrying two 90-pound *pieces*—one hung from a tumpline around the forehead and a second nestled on top—had covered the portage at a rate of about three miles an hour. That seemed about right to us. The Grand Portage should take most of an afternoon.

The voyageurs had been small men, most under five foot four. Weight was important in the canoes, and per pound a short man can carry a lot more weight than a tall man. The shorter the better.

I am six feet. Steve is six foot three. Still, with our modern equipment and lightweight canoe we figured that we should easily be able to match the voyageurs. Five hours into the portage, we began to wonder.

We set out on the trail at 2:20 in the afternoon on May 29. The first mile or so the trail rambled along smoothly. In anticipation of the pain of the portage, we had left a good deal of food and equipment with friends at the beginning of the trail. Some of this was gone for good and some would be brought to us later in the trip.

I started off carrying the canoe and the clothes pack. Steve had the gear and the food. The trail was level, the walking was not difficult, and we were enthusiastic.

When the path turned narrow and muddy, I realized that I was breathing hard. A backward glance revealed that we had been climbing steadily. Ahead, the path steepened.

By the time we reached Old Highway 61 we were exhausted and out of water. We had climbed almost eight hundred feet in the four miles, stopping only twice. We had balanced the canoe and packs well, so there was no cutting pain from pack straps or the canoe's shoulder yokes. But because of the weight of the gear I felt as if I was on a planet with five times the gravity of earth. Every movement was a struggle. As we rested on the old road, we felt the sweat drip down our necks. Silently, grimly, we prepared ourselves for the next leg.

I thought about the story that Jean Gulden had told us two days before. She had been on a portage once with an uncle who had never been canoeing. He had been struggling along the trail, puffing with exhaustion, when he saw a cow moose step on to the path. "If I'd known that they had mules," he had said, "I wouldn't have carried all this stuff."

Striding slowly down the path I let my mind wander—anything to take it away from the strain in my body. We are, by nature, land animals, and I had looked forward to this portage as a pause in the endless paddling.

The portage also marked a major benchmark of our progress and signaled the beginning of control. No longer would we be at the mercy of the lake.

But as the portage dragged on the enthusiasm evolved into a rage at the things responsible for my pain: the trip, the gear—especially Steve's gear.

And then my mind was wrenched by the thought that thousands of others had traversed this very same path in much worse circumstances. They hadn't complained. I could almost see them now as I trudged along, carrying this high-tech canoe and lightweight gear. I was doing this for fun. What would they have thought?

But they hadn't carried the gray bag. Steve's gray bag. A small duffel. I carried it in my bare hands, switching continuously from one to the other in growing aggravation. What was in the bag? It seemed to weigh a ton. I certainly didn't have anything like that along.

How could Steve have brought anything so heavy? I'd confront him the next time I saw him. I'd ask him what he was doing bringing such a heavy thing. Didn't he understand that I had the heavy load—that he was getting off easy? Why didn't he carry the gray bag for awhile? I plodded along, ready to explode with anger.

The cartographer had made a mistake. How could anyone be so careless about measuring the simple distance of a path? Surely the mapmaker meant nine miles as a crow flies, not actual distance on the path. We must already have covered a good nine miles, so why weren't we there yet? And why doesn't the park service put up markers to let us know how far we have come? Probably because they didn't want to give the game away on the guy who made the maps.

When one of the food pack straps broke I just stared at it. Too tired to stop, I simply dropped the pack and continued on.

When I caught up with Steve, we decided to start making double trips. I set my pack down and headed back to pick up the one I had left.

When I returned I walked past the other pack and continued on. I couldn't believe that I had actually carried both packs before. Nobody could be expected to shoulder a pack like this. I was still angry, and as I dropped my pack for the return trip, I seethed at the thought of Steve carrying the light packs all the time.

Even when we switched packs, the one I carried was heavier. But I resolved not to show my frustration. A smile would hide it, and I prepared to show one of my best. Just then Steve walked by. He was grinning. I knew we were in trouble.

After we crossed the place where the remnants of the old highway crossed Grand Portage, the trail leveled off, but the footing became worse. Though seldom traveled, the narrow path was a series of ruts worn deep into the soft moist ground.

Now it began to rain, and our already damp spirits plummeted to new depths. Up and down we traveled, forging through mud and muck and even plowing through a beaver pond into which the trail descended.

Although we had no way of determining how far we had come, we did know that the path branched somewhere before the river. Until we reached this fork we knew we were more than a mile from our destination. It became our worst nightmare. We had been on the trail for more than six hours and even the long spring day was giving way to darkness. Straining with our packs, we pushed on and on to get to that last bend and that fork. We must have turned a thousand bends, but the one we were desperate for never came. Push, push, push and peer ahead, let the load drop and return for the next one.

Then, finally, there was the fork. Only about a mile more to go now. Given a new strength, we pushed for the end. In the still of the darkness, treading carefully over the uneven path, we heard the rush of water and knew our labors were finally over.

The rest would be a breeze.

# CHAPTER FOUR

# Height O' Land

*Je suis un homme du nord.*
Now I, too, am a north man.

**The Boast of the Voyageur**

The Boundary Waters Canoe Area—a wilderness region in Minnesota on the U.S. side of the border with Canada—holds a special magic.

When Steve and I were growing up in Duluth, the lakes and woods of this land became the location of our earliest outdoors experiences. During our growing-up years we had made the trip to this country in family cars—though in our youthful imaginations the cars had been cleverly converted into wilderness expedition vehicles. No longer was the station wagon or Dodge Dart simply a people mover. With the canoe strapped on its roof and its back end bulging with enough gear to supply an army, it became an advanced technology cruiser. Once we stuffed our shirt pockets with Snickers bars and made that quick early morning stop at the Satellite Inn for the last evenly cooked pancakes for a week, we were on our way. A couple of hours later the canoe would be tipped from the back of the car and the adventure would begin.

On this trip, though, we had been the transport. With our own sweat we had come to the lakes and had taken the Grand Portage. It felt good.

*The border-country wilderness was the home of mosquito warfare.*

We looked forward to savoring the moment, to seeing again the beauty of trips of the past. But what we saw at portage's end was a river that wasn't any more than a large stream, its brown water not more than 20 feet wide and unappetizingly dank.

Searching for even ground, we stumbled upon a small campsite. In the glow of our flashlights we caught sight of a backpacker's red tent. We looked at each other in disbelief. A tent was the last thing we had expected to see.

Sullenly, we dropped our packs in a nearby clearing, wondering how to go about making camp. Pitching the tent was not a problem. We didn't have a tent. We had left it with friends at the beginning of the trail to cut down on weight. At the time it had seemed like a bold and good move. Now, as I wiped the rain from my face and swatted at the mosquitoes, I began to reconsider. This was the beginning of mosquito warfare.

Accomplished as we were at daylight fighting, we were but novices in the art of hand-to-hand nighttime mosquito combat. It was bloody. That first night, forced by the heat to leave the protection of our sleeping bags, we suffered casualties. Before the summer would end, though, a great number of our adversaries would meet their maker.

After perhaps six hours of non-sleep, we arose to a beautiful clear morning. Eager to get on the water, we whipped up a quick breakfast and started loading the canoe, laundering our pants in the rapids as we worked.

At the water we were met by the inhabitant of the red tent. A native of Chicago, the man had taken the bus up to Grand Portage and had hiked over the trail three times to bring in all his gear. He didn't have a boat but hoped to fish the river from the shore. He had forgotten his fishing pole on the bus. Would we be willing to sell him one of ours?

Well, if there is a person on earth who could have denied this man a fishing rod after he had suffered so much pain, I hope not to meet that person. Steve gave the camper his extra rod and wished him good luck. The man launched us. We were on our way.

Compared to the trials of the Grand Portage, paddling up the slow current of the river was child's play. The worst was behind us, we thought. Several hours later we found the first signs that we were wrong.

The water level was low, and the rapids we encountered were nearly impassable. At each patch of fast water we were forced to get out of the canoe and haul it along. In water to our knees we lurched the boat forward and struggled to retain our balance on the uneven stones beneath our feet. Often a misplaced foot slid between large rocks, threatening to wrench an ankle. Such an injury, we knew, would be disastrous, and even our heavy leather boots provided little protection.

When we reached another smooth section of river we would clamber into the boat and paddle until we were forced once again into the foaming waters.

While we paddled we were blessed with the sights of the beauty of the land and wildlife about us. To the left lay the United States; to the right, Canada. How amazing, I thought, that the river would follow so precisely the border between the two nations. Steve ventured that something more than coincidence was at work here.

As we turned a bend in water so slow that we noticed no current, we saw the first and last moose of the trip. A bull, with racks sized to the season, stood quietly in the shallows, digging in the soft bottom for the roots that sustained it. The moose was at home in the thick and tangled woods. Picking up our scent, it turned its head and broke noisily through the brush, pushing it aside as easily as we would tall grass.

Ducks were more abundant. At every turn, it seemed, we saw goldeneye mothers and their ducklings. At our approach the mother would take off, faking a broken wing and making a comical commotion in an effort to lure us away from her young.

As we progressed, the stretches of smooth water shortened and the length of the rapids increased. Not only the length, but the power too.

We tried "lining" the canoe, both of us taking a side of the river and pulling on the bow with a rope. As we went along, the river became so shallow and the gaps between the rocks so small that it became hardly worth getting back in the boat. Finally it was evident that we could no longer pull the canoe over the rocks without destroying it altogether. With no portage near us, we tied the canoe to a branch, grabbed what gear we could carry and headed inland, hoping to come to a trail or South Fowl Lake, the headwaters of the river.

After half an hour of forging through brush, I began to wonder how I could have complained about the Grand Portage. It was at least a trail. We hadn't had to plow through brush like a moose.

A moose, I thought, would have no trouble here. But we did. Branches grabbed at the packs, twigs slapped our faces and eyes, and underbrush caught our feet. Maybe it would have been better to have stayed on the river where it was clear. Where was that lake?

Finally, we saw the trees thin in the distance and could see a faint blue beyond. It was South Fowl Lake. Finding the outlet to the Pigeon River, we dropped our gear and began making our way back for the canoe.

Without the packs the going was easier, so we decided to follow the river. That way we wouldn't overshoot the boat. The banks were so overgrown, though, that the going was difficult and we were often forced into the water—partly swimming, partly wading.

When we reached the canoe, we wearily grabbed hold and started the long haul back to the lake. It would be almost impossible to carry the boat through the brush, we knew, so we dragged it up the river, often losing our footing and our grip on the canoe. We didn't even want to look at its once smooth hull.

Soaked to the skin and exhausted, we pulled the canoe onto the open lake and loaded it. The sky was clear and the sun was beginning to set over the high cliffs and green pines of the South Fowl. We were finally free to paddle on the lakes. It felt as if we'd come home.

Tomorrow we would have beautiful paddling. But, now, all I could think of was a fire and dry clothing.

On the first of June we crossed the Laurentian Divide, that point of the continent where the waters begin flowing toward the great rivers, lakes and ocean of the north. From now on we would be paddling downstream and wouldn't have to fight the current.

Traditionally, as well as geographically, the divide marks a point of transition for those paddling northward. Between the bodies of North and South Lakes, a voyageur becomes initiated into the membership of the Nor'westers of the Great Lakes. With great ceremony we found balsam boughs and sprinkled each other with water at the spot, each joining in the ancient vow not to kiss another voyageur's wife without her permission and not to let another pass without the same ceremony.

The voyageurs, we had been told, had also held to the tradition of draining their unwieldy kegs of rum at this spot. I think that if Steve and I had had a keg, we would have finished it at about the time the pack strap broke on Grand Portage.

In addition to being initiated we were truly refreshed. The day before the rain had left us, and the wind had come up enough in the evening to keep the bugs off us as we slept. The paddling was easy and the fishing was good. Even the two-mile portage into Rose Lake hadn't seemed so bad in comparison with the struggles we had already endured. Early summer in the Boundary Waters was welcoming us. We could have lived that life forever.

Later that afternoon we paddled on through to Gunflint Lake and stopped at Gunflint Lodge to stock up on food. After a good dinner and an exchange of stories with canoe guide Karl Johnson that lasted deep into the night, we pushed off late and with flashlights found a spot to camp. By this time we were becoming more adept at setting up our Spartan camp. The bags were out on the ground in no time.

We set off the next morning along the Granite River, one of the most beautiful stretches of water we had ever seen. For the first time we were actually helped by the current, and we enjoyed the excitement of the short rapids.

Our goal was Canada Customs on Saganaga Lake. We knew we'd have to hurry to get there before Customs closed, and to make time we experimented with different stroke rates. We tried the rapid one I'd seen the Canadians use—with switches every 10 strokes—but found it not to our liking. Instead, we fell into a steady and even pace, switching sides regularly but not often. The rate, we found, increased with every day we paddled.

Late in the afternoon, as we were thrown by the river into the arms of Red Sucker Bay on Saganaga, we noticed the darkening of the skies overhead. We hurried the canoe toward Government Island, on which the Customs office stood.

We couldn't beat the weather. The sky blackened and met the lake with sheets of rain. We were drenched before we could pull out the rain gear, which was placed strategically at the bottom of the packs. Even after we managed to get the rain suits on, the thin nylon shells provided little protection. Waves of water found their way to our shivering bodies.

Drawing upon a small portion of the reserves of blind luck that we enjoyed calling navigation, we threaded our way through a maze of islands, coming eventually upon a waving Canadian flag, its red maple leaf marking the outpost. We walked up the floating wooden dock, after tying up carefully away from the float plane moorings. To our left was an old aluminum boat with the words CUSTOMS and DOUANES painted in black upon the sides. Ahead, we saw the same words on a large wooden sign, its worn edges and faded lettering bearing silent witness to life in northern weather.

Several paces up the wooden decking sat the small cabin that served as both the Customs office and the living quarters for the ranger on duty. A propane tank provided fuel for the post's few comforts. Because this was considered a hardship post, its rangers were rotated every 10 days, switching between this island and the Pigeon River border station along Lake Superior.

White with a neat red trim, the cabin neatly fit the character of the woods. On the door we saw that office hours ended at seven. We hoped we weren't too late.

"It's after nine now, boys," said the graying and grizzled ranger as we walked through the door, "but I guess that doesn't mean so much up here."

"My name's Don," he continued, "Why don't you just have a seat while I get out the forms."

We found out later that Don had worked at the station most of his life and was about to retire. He couldn't have been more helpful.

When we explained our intentions, Don looked out the window, incredulously eyeing our outfit. "Good luck," he said as he wrote out an entry permit for three months: vehicle of entry—canoe.

Noting the threatening skies, we asked Don if he might know of a good place to camp. He suggested one of any number of nearby islands. It wasn't quite what we had hoped to hear. We were more specific. Might he know of a good place to camp with a lot of shelter for a couple of wet guys who didn't have a tent?

Don scratched his head and said that he really couldn't say. But on the other side of the island there was an old ranger's cabin that had been abandoned. He figured it might just be possible that the door had been left unlocked.

"Too bad you guys weren't here a couple weeks ago," he said, "the Young Rangers stayed there—about 20 young ladies volunteering their time for the summer to pick up garbage around the lakes." Yeah, too bad.

# CHAPTER FIVE

# Kawnipi

*And a verse of a Lapland song is haunting my memory still . . .*
*A boy's will is the winds's will*
*And the thoughts of youth are long, long thoughts . . .*

**Longfellow**

The next day, the third of June, we awoke to a strong wind out of the north.

This forced us to hug close to the string of islands along the northwestern side of Saganaga. Eventually we would have to cross open water to reach our destination of the Quetico Provincial Park ranger station in Cache Bay, but our Lake Superior experiences had taught us to respect the wind.

After several hours of back-breaking paddling I realized that I had left my fishing rod at the cabin where we had said goodbye to Don. Frustrated, we returned over the distance we had struggled so hard to cover.

Later, heading once more to the west, we found ourselves forced to buck the wind and waves to make a jump between two islands. It was that or be pushed farther south out of our way. We decided to give it a try.

With the spray cover firmly in place, we sent the canoe into the waves. The swells were greater than we had expected. Without the

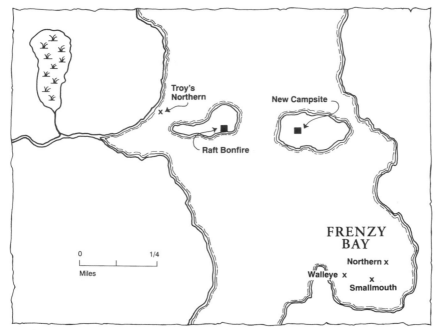

*Fishing spots on Frenzy Bay may or may not be accurately marked.*

spray cover and the skills we had gained on Lake Superior, I don't think we would have made it across.

An hour later we reached the shelter of an island but found ourselves pushed way off course. As it turned out, we were near islands on which three friends and I had camped at the end of a trip many years earlier. Our food had run out, and we had had to wait there on the island for three days until our parents were due to show up. The Quetico Survivors, we had called ourselves. Looking out across the whitecaps, I hoped that the name would apply equally well this time.

Steve and I spent the night on an island not two miles from the ranger station at Cache Bay, pinned down again by the weather. The next morning an early calm gave us the chance we needed. Gliding quickly across the smooth water that only the night before had been impassable, we came upon the station.

After climbing the steep path to the cabin, we signed the log book and picked up our permits and fishing licenses. The rangers—a married couple with a small child—had been working at the station for five summers. They wintered a thousand miles away in Newfoundland, but the Quetico was like home to them.

It was from them that we learned about the Atikokan trans-Quetico canoe race. For years the race had pitted canoe teams of the U.S. against Canadians. Competition had grown so fierce that each side had resorted to trickery. To buy valuable time, some competitors had slipped into the lakes before the beginning of the race and had cut false portages. After running several hundred yards into the woods with canoe and gear, the duped team would see the trail end abruptly and be forced to turn around. Now the race skirts the park.

We told the rangers about our trip and explained that we had decided to cut through Quetico instead of continuing along the border route. When we asked about river conditions on two alternate routes, they radioed a ranger at the far end of the park. He said that it was about an even choice between the Maligne River and the Beaverhouse, but that he would probably choose the latter.

As we prepared to push off into the drizzle, the rangers once again explained that we were to head straight north up to Cache Bay, keeping a large pine to our left and a small island to our right. We would know the right channel by a large bluff. "Whatever you do," they said, "don't bear too far to the left. Half the canoeists do and end up in Lost Bay."

It sounded ominous, but I assured them that I had been to Cache Bay before and that we weren't stupid and wouldn't go the wrong way.

Lost Bay, it turned out, actually was very nice. Still, we were in a hurry so we paddled right back out until we found a channel with a large bluff.

As a general note to novice canoeists, I should say that it is important in such circumstances to throw out your fishing lines as soon as possible. This gives observers the illusion that your every turn or backtrack is meticulously planned to coincide with the movements of a school of walleyes. Veteran paddlers do this by habit. By the end of the trip it was instinctive for us, and we would throw out the lines even before we pulled out the maps.

Eventually we reached Silver Falls. The portage around it, tricky even on good days, was treacherous and wet. It was full of boulders and drop-offs. The going was slow, and each step was made with care. By the end of the portage we were soaked from pushing through the water-laden brush.

As we loaded the boat and started out, we passed by a group of paddlers decked out in the latest high-tech outer garments. Scoffing at their weakness, I sat up a bit straighter to reposition the layers of my sopping shirt and jacket.

After sloshing through several muddy portages, we came to the Falls Chain, a series of waterfalls between Saganagons and Kawnipi. Four years before I had been there when a man had drowned in the fast water. But now the water was down a good three feet, judging by the shore markings. We should be OK as long as we didn't take too many chances.

Along the chain we took time out to take some pictures of an otter family. In a calm section of river we had seen three river otters poke their heads from the water. Every time I tried to shoot them, the little guys dove before the shutter snapped, and we found ourselves chasing them up and down the river.

Once we thought we had them cornered. We had forced them back into a small bay housing a large beaver lodge. The otters dove again. Waiting quietly for them to surface, we were startled by a thundering splash in front of the boat. It was the beaver! Listening, we heard the otters scratching around inside the lodge. Who would have thought it?

By the time we arrived at Lake Kawnipi the weather had cleared and the sun was poking through the clouds as it began its descent. At the end of the last portage we had stopped to talk to some people on their way out. Fishing had been pretty good, they said. Especially the walleye.

Three times I had come to Kawnipi and each time I felt it had marked a distinct period in my life. Kawnipi—long and narrow, with as many extending bays as the weather has changes—was the home of some of my fondest memories.

We paddled into it that day and up to a favorite camping space. Old times came rushing back.

I recalled that, when I was 17, some friends and I had camped at the island for three days—trying to understand life and our new-found freedom.

I could see vividly the 22-pound northern that Troy had caught and the look on his face as he did.

Osto had turned 18 at that campsite and we had made him a no-bake cheese cake topped with chocolate pudding.

I remembered the raft we made. How we had worked all day gathering logs and lashing them with rope into a marvel of naval architecture. I have a picture of us standing on the raft, its timbers sinking slowly, our ankles disappearing into the water.

We burned the raft and sat for hours around the flames discussing deeply the secret things 17-year-olds discuss around a fire in the deep woods.

We talked about the future, which at that time meant the coming football season. There would be life after that, we knew, and graduation—but we could not stretch our minds into such a void of abstraction.

We talked about ourselves and about a past we had just so recently broken from. As if inevitable, the conversation turned to UFOs. Even the staunchest disbeliever begins to wonder out there in the woods.

"I'm not saying they're real," Troy explained, "but it just seems that there are a lot of things that we don't know about . . . ."

Actually, at 17 there were a lot of other things we didn't know about either—and probably still don't. But we thought we knew.

We talked about God, too, as we stared into the bright stars above, pondering and questioning. A cool breeze brought the smell of the fire and of the lake, and a feeling of life surged about. The questions remained, but answers were all around.

The next morning Mike and I had got up early to fish the shallow bay where Troy had caught the big fish. It started to pour, but we sat in the rain for hours trying to equal the catch of our friend. I wanted to go in, few things displeasing me as much as sitting in a canoe fishing in the rain, but Mike wouldn't hear of it.

I wonder if Mike would do the same today. I think he would.

Two years later I took my dad and brother to the island. I had just finished my first year at college and had a couple of weeks of vacation before I started a job in the city for the summer. I remember feeling that I had sold out. I would spend the summer in a suit and tie, living in an office in a city. What kind of life was that?

We found some great fishing spots that trip. We called the best one Frenzy Bay—water so alive with fish that we had cut the barbs off our hooks just to ease the task of releasing the fish.

The next year my dad broke the trust of our secret lake. Betraying the timeless vow taken by all fishermen, Dad took friends of his to the spot—without asking our permission. The fishing was lousy. Lakes always know.

Steve and I built a great fire that first night on Kawnipi. No raft to burn this time, just a cold night to welcome.

I told Steve that we should go through Kawnipi because of the great fishing—because of the 22-pound northern, the 5-pound smallmouth and, of course, Frenzy Bay.

But I knew that that wasn't the real reason I kept going back. I returned because of the little marsh where we had followed the moose, the stars in the sky and the glow of the fires—fires so bright I often saw them in my mind's eye late into the winter.

Kawnipi had become a measuring stick of my life. This time I thought of how much I had changed in the years that had passed. And wondered how much I would change before I returned. Could we ever get back to the freedom of spirit we had possessed on that island when we were 17?

Breaking the silence, Steve stirred the fire. "You know," he said, "I'm not committing to anything, but it just seems sort of unreasonable that in the whole universe we would be the only kind of life . . . ."

# CHAPTER SIX

# Call Me Ishmeal

*One should be careful to get out of an
experience only the wisdom that is in it,
lest we be like the cat that sits on the hot stove lid.
She will never sit on a hot stove lid again,
and that's well; but also she will never sit
on a cold one anymore.*

**Mark Twain**

We quickened our paddling in the Quetico, strengthened our stroke and gained a knowledge of what we could do in the canoe.

A brief shower didn't dampen our spirits. We simply took out the plastic bags that Don had given us at the Customs office, cut holes for our arms and legs and put the bags over our wool shirts.

The day after leaving Kawnipi, a few hours of work brought us to Russell Lake. This lake, blessed with an abundance of sandy beaches and thundering falls, must be one of the most picturesque lakes in all of the Quetico. Not far from the portage into Russell, I found a moose horn stuck high in the branches of a balsam. I decided to bring it along. Although heavy and awkward to carry, it added an important new element to the appearance of camp and canoe.

We passed through Russell on June 6. We had said that we would be at Namakan Lake by the 10th. We were headed for an island retreat that is owned by friends of the family, Dick and Cecile

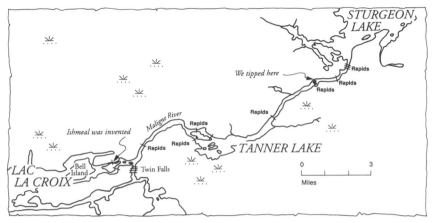

*The Maligne proved to be as malevolent as its name.*

Swenson. Our plan called for them dropping off fresh supplies for us there. That gave us four days to cover the 60 miles to the island. We could easily have covered that distance in half that time.

Two nights later we woke to the sound of a light rain falling on the tarp over our heads. We had decided to take a couple of layover days and had camped on Blueberry Island in Sturgeon Lake, where we were trying our hands at fishing. We had found a really nice bare rock island and had set up camp on its clean face. The fish, however, would not bite.

Steve is not one to give up easily. Baring himself, he made a vain attempt to commune completely with the spirit of the fish. However noble the effort, naked fishing did not work.

The rain was doing its work, though—telling us that it was time to move on.

We had packed our gear and promised ourselves that we would shove off as soon as the rain started in earnest—even if it was in the middle of the night. If we were going to be wet, we said, we might as well be moving. We had even cooked up a batch of biscuits in anticipation of a quick departure. We expected a full day of hard paddling without stopping even to cook—a biscuit day; a B.D.

Steve slept through the arrival of the rain. Not wanting to wake him, I grabbed more of the cover we had laid over our bags and tried to roll it in. I'd just wait until he woke up.

Tarps are notoriously finite. Steve seemed to grasp this concept and he wrenched on the plastic, still sleeping deeply. If I had been fully awake I would have got out of my warm, dry bag and loaded the canoe in the dark, cold rain. But sleep was still appealing.

Once again, applying an even pressure to our mutual protection, I managed to cover a good half of my body and some of our gear, too, as the light rain turned into a downpour.

Finally, we roused ourselves and set off, filled with grand ideas of making the 60 miles. If we paddled all day, we thought, we might just be able to reach the meeting point before dark. It was worth a try.

We planned on paddling down Sturgeon Lake to its southwest end and into the mouth of the Maligne River. The ranger had told us that if we decided on the Maligne, although the water was low, we might be able to cover most of the river without a portage. Some spots would be tricky, he had said, but we should be able to make it through. Of course this was the same guy who had cut all the blind portages for the Americans.

The Maligne emptied into Lac LaCroix. We would travel up that large border lake and then sneak into the Namakan River, which we would follow to Namakan Lake and our meeting place.

As we pushed the canoe toward our destination, conversation—as on every morning—was slow in coming. It seemed that our minds, like our bodies, had to be warmed into activity. So I do not blame Steve for not recalling from his French studies that *maligne* actually means "wicked" in that language. Besides, three hours later, I figured it out for myself.

Because we were relatively new to river canoeing, we decided to stop at the top of every set of rapids and scout for possible problems. We would then decide whether to try our luck on the water or make the carry.

The first fast water was an obvious portage. We landed at a clearing upstream of the first whitewater and made our way 30 yards downstream. The rest of the stretch was worth paddling. Loading the gear and strapping it securely into the boat, we worked our way into the stream, the current pulling steadily at our canoe. Paddling backward to maintain control and position, we scouted a route and prepared ourselves for what was to come.

We slid down the cascading fall. Our excitement grew.

When we hit the first rock I realized that, other attributes aside, a Kevlar canoe is to be praised for the stoic courage with which it withstands impact.

An aluminum boat, as if to tell all the world of its agony, screams and whines when it runs over some submerged obstacle. Then, as a lasting remembrance, it paints a silver monument to its pain as it passes by.

Kevlar stands the test with nothing more than a murmur, leaving only a slight trace as it sheds its skin in the interest of progress.

With the murmur of Kevlar in my ears, I shifted my weight and pushed with my paddle against the current, trying to dislodge our stranded vessel. Steve pulled, and soon we were free and gliding once again. Several encounters later we were past the rapids and on our way downstream.

After several more miles we came upon a short but steep section of rapids. Splitting into three sections around two small islands, the river dropped about four feet into a small pool. We pulled up to one of the islands to look at possible routes. We ruled out immediately the left and middle branches. They were nothing less than small waterfalls and would have been impossible to navigate. The channel to our right looked more promising. The water was smooth except for a standing wave halfway down on the left. If we could keep the canoe to the right of the wave we would have a clear shot.

Our other option was a portage across the island we were standing on. This would have taken no more than five minutes. But, spurred on by the excitement of the river we had just paddled, we eyed the passage intently.

Remembering the advice that naturalist Sigurd Olson had given us several months before, we decided to give it a shot. "You're going to have to handle some pretty heavy whitewater up north," he had told us. "Lots to learn—both you and the boat. Better do it somewhere that you can afford the lessons."

This seemed like a good place to start, and besides, we needed to save time if we wanted to make the 60 miles.

I believe that it is in a person's nature to exert considerable effort to avoid labor and save time. This thought ran through my mind during the 20 minutes it took us to secure the gear in the canoe. With the splash cover wrapped tightly about our waists we took one last look at the flume below us and plunged into the raging waters.

Some seconds later I realized that the time we had spent designing the quick-release mechanism of the spray cover had been unnecessary. Under certain circumstances almost any design converts to quick-release. Being strapped in an overturned canoe was one of those circumstances, and Steve and I proved adequately that at such a time a quick thrust against the canoe bottom turns the entire spray cover into a release mechanism.

Somehow we had been sucked into the left side of the current and had learned all too well that the standing wave was not just a strange phenomenon of nature, but was actually caused by a rock hidden by the swiftly moving water.

After the initial shock wore off and we realized that we had both escaped unharmed, we began laughing and pulled the canoe to one of the banks of the river. After we reached shore we took stock of the price we had paid for our adventure. I had lost my paddle when we swamped and swam to recover it from the eddy upstream in which it was swirling. All our gear was soaked, and Steve had lost his glasses. It would be contact lenses from then on.

By the time we wrung out our gear it was midafternoon. The air, which had seemed so balmy an hour before, chilled our bodies. Without dry clothes it seemed that we might never get warm. We had to keep moving.

As the sun sank we pushed down the river. In the cool air it seemed that our woolen shirts would never dry nor warmth return to our bodies. At Eva Island at the end of the Maligne, we realized that we would have to stop for the night. A fire would warm our shaking bodies and dry our gear.

Steve gathered firewood and I took stock of our food supplies. Though it had been wrapped in protective plastic, little had survived the drenching. It was good that we were only a day away from the supplies that our friends were to have left for us at their cabin on Namakan.

Until that time we had been eating mostly macaroni and cheese, pancakes and rice. We had brought along macaroni and had found that it was a perfect food for shoveling carbohydrates into our bodies. Practicing and perfecting one-pot cooking, we would usually boil the rice or pasta in a large pot and then add cheese if it was macaroni or some sort of animal bouillon if it was rice. We had few rules for the latter, but we never mixed our animals.

Steve came back with some wood and I put the water to a boil, throwing in some of the sopping rice. I added what was left of the dried peas and millet. As if overcome by an irresistible force, I grabbed a couple of packs of chicken noodle soup and tossed them into the brew. When I reached for the lentils and curry powder I knew that I was no longer controlling my own actions. Grabbing for the remaining pancake mix and pouring it into the pot, I called out to Steve for help. But he was already back in the woods, too far to hear my hysterical cries.

By the time Steve returned I had gained control and was beginning to think clearly. Empty bags were all around me. The carrots, the beef boullion, the raisins, the GRAPE-NUTS; they were all gone.

"What're you making?" Steve innocently asked as he glanced into the pot.

The answer, coming from somewhere deep within the pot itself, rose hoarsely to my trembling lips. "Ishmeal."

# CHAPTER SEVEN

# Namakan Moon, Underwear Fires

*Today we'll have a
change of underwear.
B Company, change
with C Company.*

**Bob Baker**

Wᵉ burned our underwear on the 10th of June.

We had tried everything but couldn't save them. Sadly we prepared a funeral pyre for the garments that had served us so well over the difficult times that lay behind us.

The clothes went up like kindling, carrying with them our memories of the trials through which we had passed. Luckily we had picked up three new pair with our fresh supplies.

The day before we had covered the remaining 30 miles to our destination small island on Namakan Lake. Paddling well into the evening to reach our goal, we were rewarded with one of the most beautiful scenes we had ever seen. Though the sun had been lost long before, the water was illuminated still by the silver light of an enormous moon. The only sound came from our paddles as they pulled at the still water.

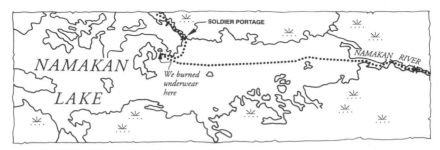

*Here the unbefitting underwear fueled a malodorous pyre.*

The islands around us, eerie in the vague outlines of their silhouettes, seemed to float on the black water. Their tree-lined hills, stunning in the daylight, were majestic in the moonglow. Across the lake we could make out the warm glow of a distant fire.

Soon we reached our island. We spent several days there, resting and repairing our equipment. We dried our gear, replenished our food supply from the cache that had been left for us and gave the canoe a fresh coat of Fiberglas to smooth the bottom we had worn so ragged.

We also added an old worn guitar to our gear. The tent that we had left behind at Grand Portage was back with us, too. Saunas and swims completed the physical rejuvenation.

When we finally left, a new set of maps guided us to the Soldier Portage that linked Namakan to its northern neighbor, Rainy Lake. Soldier Portage, a short carry, ended at a small stream feeding into Rainy Lake. Though passable in wetter years, the stream was so low that we were forced to portage almost its entire length so as not to scratch the newly refinished canoe. We were finally rewarded with the dark hues of Rainy Lake. Now we had a clear paddle for at least 80 miles.

As we pulled out into the small bay, we were greeted at once by a fair headwind. With the wind in our faces, at least we knew that we were going in the right direction. Without this headwind to guide us we might well have been lost for days in the intricate maze of islands that dot Rainy Lake.

With its many hidden rocks, sunken islands and frequent high winds, Rainy Lake can be treacherous—for those in motorboats because of the danger of high-speed encounters with the rocks, and for those in canoes because of the winds.

Paddling only as far as the lake's main open expanse, we were forced to take cover on an island, waiting for the cool night to bring an end to the wind's reign over our craft. Stranded there on our fortress of rock, we felt the strength of the wind and knew it could not harm us. Instead it drove from us the flies and mosquitoes and provided background to our songs, now accompanied by our guitar.

The wind caught the words and pulled them away even as they left our mouths.

As the sun sank beyond the horizon, we left the island and paddled for several hours toward the dark distant shore. Finding ourselves entangled in a labyrinth of islands, we decided that it would be better to camp rather than paddle, more likely than not, in the wrong direction. With flashlights in hand, we discovered a small clearing on an island and threw down our sleeping bags.

The next morning we found our way with some difficulty to navigational buoys marking passage to International Falls and Fort Frances, the border communities made famous by their winter weather reports.

Gliding over boulders only inches from the surface, we pitied those people who had to travel the waters in a powerboat. In this low water, going was hazardous.

It was strange to see the homes and docks and people that lined the shores of the lake. We had come to know the silence of the waters and knew that civilization was a stranger to it. Traveling by our own power, at a slow pace, we had begun to comprehend the true dimensions of the lakes and the woods and the islands.

It was time that meant the most to us. Given enough time, we could cover any distance and do anything. Speed meant nothing. The people who came from the cities to grab a quick weekend on the water needed their fast boats and cars to cover their distances. They went as far in a day as we would have in 10. But then, we had the 10—and the silence.

When we stopped that night it was too dark to find a good camping site. Earlier we had pulled along the shoreline of Fort Frances and there had met Clint and Janie enjoying the summer evening from high atop their dock. Clint was a cop. Janie worked at the photo shop. They invited us up for a cold drink. By the time we had left, the sun was already going down.

At Fort Frances we had strayed from the conventional course to Lake of the Woods. Instead of following along the Rainy River, which connects Rainy Lake directly to Lake of the Woods, we had decided to follow an obscure chain of lakes that would carry us from the very northwest corner of Rainy Lake, through Kakagi and Caviar Lakes and into a northeastern bay of Lake of the Woods. That way we hoped to avoid a lot of power boats and to have some good fishing.

We paddled about an hour before pulling up to an island. Not wanting to set up the tent we had picked up at Namakan, we threw our sleeping bags out on their pads and prepared ourselves for the bugs. Slipping inside fully clothed, we donned gloves and head nets. They didn't help.

It is hard to sleep when a bloody death is buzzing only two inches from your face. Try as we might, we could not quite shut out the roar of that thirsty mass. When we did manage to nod off, our faces would touch the protective net and a thousand invaders would instantly attack.

Additional layers of clothing were not the answer. The warm night made them equally uncomfortable. Besides, mosquitoes are smarter than people; so regardless of technological disadvantage, a few will find their way through as many as four layers of pants and into the bottom reaches of a sleeping bag. The occupant in there is powerless.

There was only one sure revenge on these animals. The Swat. But even then they had the last laugh. I wonder how we would have looked that night from a distance, thrashing about at random intervals, repeatedly smashing our heads with gloved and bundled hands.

When morning finally, mercifully, arrived, we fled that horrid island. Once free, we must have paddled a good half hour before daring to remove the headgear that protected us from the blood-thirsty horde.

After another two hours we felt that it would be safe to stop for some breakfast. We stopped at an island and, going back to the water to make some Tang, we noticed that the lake was laden with a different sort of bug. These were dead and, looking like some sort of scorpion-dragon combination with a needle-like tail, they were five times the size of the mosquito. It was mayfly time.

Because we were from Minnesota, we were used to the hatching and, more obnoxious, the dying of the mayflies. Once a summer, millions of the insects come teeming up from the depths of the waters, gradually grow, go to college, get a job, find another eye-grabbing mayfly and start a big mayfly family. This completed, all within 24 hours, they give up their lives and sink back into the waters to provide a blanket of nourishment for walleyes and bass. They also provide a great deal of consternation to anglers and those wanting to swim in, drink out of, or simply enjoy the lake.

In Canada, we learned, the creatures are called fishflies. It wasn't the only example of Canadians and Yanks using different words we would note, but this one particularly bothered us. At least the name mayfly hinted that after May, maybe in June or at the latest early July, the bugs would be gone. At home this had been true.

In Canada it was not. Apparently, as the summer progressed, the hatch moved farther and farther north. Unfortunately, so did we.

Tired and thirsty, Steve searched for a clear patch on the water. Finding none, he contented himself with brushing a part of the mass out of the way and scooping quickly with the pot he held.

After breakfast we paddled on toward Rainy Lake. As we made our way through the organisms on the surface, we were hailed by a young man in a powerboat. A native of Fort Frances, he worked for a man who was building a house on one of the islands. The boat, an older model Fiberglas runabout with a 50-horse outboard, belonged to his employer.

Eyeing the American flags on the side of our canoe, he asked where we were from. "Duluth," we answered.

"Where'd you put in?"

"Duluth."

He couldn't believe it. He said the only canoeing he had done had been on a 40-mile trip across Rainy Lake to raise money for charity. They had covered the distance in three days. "But we had a good time," he explained.

We tried to tell him that what we were doing really wasn't that hard. He didn't believe us. Deep down, I think we didn't want him to.

When we finally released our grip on his boat, he pointed out the direction we should go and took one last look at us. Then, in the salute of Canada we were growing to appreciate, he bid us goodbye. "Have a nice trip, eh!" he called. Then he gunned the throttle and was gone.

# CHAPTER EIGHT

# River's Edge

*Get thee out of thy country,*
*And from thy kindred,*
*And from thy father's house,*
*Unto a land that I will show thee.*

**Genesis 12:1**

Wh  hen we turned the corner we realized that something was wrong.

At the divide back in the Boundary Waters we had celebrated the fact that our upstream paddling was behind us. But this river wasn't dropping from us—it was rushing toward us. Quickly, we checked our maps. What we saw was like a bad dream. We had, in fact, picked out a course that led back upstream. How could we have been so stupid?

Sullenly, we emptied the boat and began lugging it up and over the rocks that crowded the shallow streambed.

Five rapids and a good deal of sweat later, we struggled up a short portage around a six-foot waterfall. Freed at last from the mayflies by the swift water, we couldn't resist the temptation to jump headlong into the falls. We found footholds in the rocks below and pulled our aching bodies into the steady surge of the falling water. This was more like it.

For four days we worked our way through chains of Ontario lakes.

*Keewatin—land of the northwest wind.*

Though we saw few people, each portaging place was marked with the aluminum fishing boats of sometime inhabitants and fishing guides. Although these vessels pointed out our trail, they did little to enhance the landscape.

On June 18 we cut our first portage. Though only a few yards long, it gave us a great deal of satisfaction to hew our way through the woods in true explorer fashion. Unfortunately, we broke the ax in the effort.

The night before we had almost needed it to carve out a place for our sleeping bags. We had crossed one last portage just as the sun was setting, hoping to make camp at the other end. Before finding the portage we had searched for it for at least an hour through the dense brush. Vainly we had pursued several game trails before realizing we had passed over the route.

When we finally did reach the lake the ground was too forested or too uneven for a sleeping spot. In almost total darkness we scanned the entire shore, hoping for a place where we could bed down. It looked like we might be spending our first night in the canoe.

Luckily, we happened upon a small clearing and were able to throw up the tent, sweating profusely as we worked. When the last gear was inside we made fast the screen door and lay reveling in the cool breeze. Suddenly my body began to tingle and itch. Steve felt the same way. Soon we realized that, though we had protected ourselves from the ravenous mosquitoes, we were still subject to the no-seeums that squeezed through the small holes in our screening. Reluctantly we closed the outer rain door and languished in the heat and stench from our own bodies.

The next day, after we had pushed through our newly made portage, the sight of the cool blue waters of Kakagi had a singularly refreshing effect. A steady wind had freed the main body from its mayfly covering and we longed to throw our bodies into the water. We got the chance. A 30-foot cliff hung out over the water's edge on an island we had to pass anyway. The water was deep, the runway clear. Ten minutes later we were hurtling our bodies off into space and plunging into the cool water.

We made Lake of the Woods the next day. Camped at a beautiful sand beach, we woke to the smell of bacon frying. Looking around us, we soon realized that the smell was coming from the kitchen of a passing houseboat. Without any means of comparison, the cold macaroni and cheese we were eating from the pot had been passable.

With this new aroma in our nostrils we just stared at the pasta in disgust.

Two hours later we were in Kenora, downing chocolate milk-shakes and submarine sandwiches. When we pulled in to the town we stopped first at the dockside laundromat and piled our soiled garments into the heavy-duty washing machines. It wouldn't help the clothes, we knew, but we had to make the effort.

With the dirty clothes in the wash, we wandered over to the grocery store. At the meat counter we met Bill Vivian, the butcher. Marveling over the tremendous selection of bacon, we were glad to have some advice from an expert. Bill, it turned out, had been a butcher for many years. Just recently, however, he had acquired a small resort down the river a couple of miles in Keewatin. He invited us to spend the night there. "It's easy to find, eh," he said, "just a couple miles past the 50-foot statue of Huskie the Muskie by the side of the river. Can't miss it."

The muskie was right where he said it would be. The river was not. Our first clue was the chain of three huge logs that had been positioned to section off the mouth of the channel. Not being easily dismayed, we found a widening of the gaps in the booms and, balancing precariously on the slippery logs, pulled the canoe across. We dried quickly in the afternoon sun.

Just in time we realized we were in the forebay of a hydroelectric dam. With effort, we turned the canoe and paddled with all our might against the quickening current. Hugging the wall-like bank, we were able to escape the river but not before I snapped the tip off my fishing rod. Looking back at the foaming water, we realized that it had been a small price to pay.

Our mistake, we decided, was that we had taken directions from a man who drives his car to cover the distance we had to paddle. It just isn't the same. We would know better next time.

After questioning some boaters we learned that we needed to continue down the shore another few miles. There we could either carry the canoe down to the river or take advantage of the boat lift. It wasn't a difficult decision.

We positioned the canoe over the rows of wooden slats and watched as the huge electric motors winched the cargo out of the water. Slowly, the lift rolled along its guides and positioned our canoe over the swirling river, easing it gently a couple of dozen feet down until it sat once more in the water. We had arrived at our first real river.

The United Church of Canada was established in 1925. It brought together several Protestant denominations in the country and formed a framework for religious activity in the remote areas of Canada.

We had our first encounter with the church the day after we left Lake of the Woods. Although we slept in the tent we enjoyed the other accommodations of the resort and awoke clean and refreshed. Realizing that it was Sunday, we decided to attend worship at a church in the local community of Keewatin.

At 11 o'clock we decked ourselves in the best of our deteriorating garments and walked the mile to the St. Andrew's UCC. We were presentable if we kept our jackets on, but in the heavy heat and humidity that didn't seem likely. It also seemed a bit strange to be wearing heavy work boots to church. But we comforted ourselves with the thought that in church nobody would notice our appearance.

"Been working out in the bush?" a lady asked politely as she turned in her seat to greet us.

We explained that we hadn't exactly been working but we had been out in the woods for quite awhile. Seemingly fascinated by our story, she nudged the man beside her and related it to him. He introduced himself as Chuck Davidson. The woman was his wife, Meg Davidson. In the few minutes before the service began we were given the chance to unburden our story and we did so.

When the organ began playing we settled down once more into the smooth wooden pews. With us in the rough hewn wooden sanctuary were perhaps 60 people. Many of them were Masons, celebrating their centennial and sweating heavily in their thick wool uniforms and hats. We, too, were suffering from the heat, and I had to remove my bright red jacket and reveal the soiled T-shirt it had been hiding.

The pastor came in and asked if there were any announcements or visitors. Unexpectedly Meg stood up and proclaimed that two fine young men had traveled a great distance by canoe to be with them. We wondered who they might be.

The sermon that day was particularly appropriate for canoeists bound for Hudson Bay. Opening with a Kipling poem praising a life on the edge of society, the pastor continued on to describe Abraham's journey of faith into the wilderness. Without Kevlar, Gore-tex or even white gas, Abraham had ventured into unknown and hostile lands simply in response to God's will and in complete trust. Compared to Abraham, we had been living the lives of kings and had complained about it daily. We would keep Abraham in mind.

When the service ended we turned to leave. As we did Chuck and Meg caught our arms and asked if we wouldn't like to have lunch with them. We tried to explain that we already had planned a nice dinner of macaroni and cheese, but Meg wouldn't hear of it. They seemed pretty set on buying us lunch, so we went along. Sometimes you just have to do that for people.

Excitedly we tumbled into the waiting car and were whisked off to dinner. It had been more than a month since we had felt such speed, and it amazed us.

Dinner was wonderful—both the food and the conversation— and we were entertained with stories of the many experiences the Davidsons had lived through in the small community.

Meg had spent a great deal of time working with UCC programs. A few years back, she and several others from her congregation had flown north to the Norway House settlement to work with the church there.

"You'll love Norway House," she said. "Make sure you stop in at the church there. Super people."

Driving back to our canoe after dinner, I could almost see young Meg leading her horse by a rope along those same streets as she delivered groceries for her father during the Depression. The streets of Keewatin had never carried a teeming population like Kenora's, but they were filled with tradition and meaning.

Actually, the larger Kenora had taken its name from Keewatin— at least partly. The "Ke" had been taken from the beginning of

Keewatin, the "no" was from the nearby settlement of Norman, and the "ra" from Rat Portage.

Keewatin itself came from an Indian word meaning "land of the northwest wind." Pulling out on the river later that afternoon, it didn't take us long to figure out why.

# CHAPTER NINE

# Dam Portages

*I hate them.*

**Steve Baker**

When I think back on our trip down the Winnipeg River, I remember the dam portages.

Not that there weren't distractions. Once we had stopped to play golf. I lost eight balls, most of which were mysteriously sucked down onto the train tracks near the second hole. A young boy on a bike had watched us from the bushes and offered to sell me used balls. Indignant, I refused. Two holes and five balls later, he was back. He gave me a pretty good deal.

But more than anything I recall the dam portages. We must have crossed a dozen of them and each portage seemed worse. The dam jokes got worse, too, but we couldn't have stopped them even if we had wanted to.

One of the worst dam portages came at Pointe du Bois. The day before, we had crossed into Manitoba and, as if on cue, a stiff northwest wind had come up to greet us. Actually the wind came from the northwest only when the river happened to be going in that direction. When the river bent to the east or the west the wind switched accordingly. Now, as we approached the massive concrete structure at Pointe du Bois we were pleased at least by the windbreak it gave us.

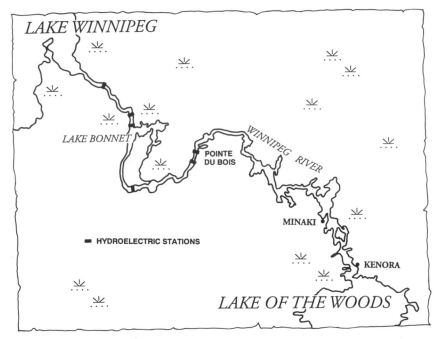

*The Winnipeg River tested the trekkers with one dam portage after another.*

Supplying power to the city of Winnipeg, Pointe du Bois and the other stations along the river were operated remotely from the city via microwave communications. Only a handful of operators were kept at the site to take care of maintenance. This posed problems for canoeists because the gates could open unexpectedly, transforming a once-sedate channel into foaming turbulence. We had to be careful.

Luckily, water levels were so low that few of the turbines were being operated. Thus the current in front of the dam was considerably less dangerous than it could have been. Still, we always went ashore well upstream of the gates to avoid the main current, which wanted to sweep us into the turbines.

By June 25 we were experts at the dam routine. The night before we had camped at a small island only a couple of miles up from the Seven Sister's Dam. Though the island was covered with thousands of the dreaded fishflies, we had holed up there to sleep off a day of paddling straight into the wind. When we awoke we scraped off the half inch of organic mass as best we could and tossed our gear into the canoe. It, too, was filled with the bugs.

As usual we scanned the shore to determine which side would give us a better landing. "It looks like we'd have a dam good chance on the right over there!" yelled Steve.

"Dam right!" I shouted back, and began turning the boat.

After we landed the canoe we pulled it up, grabbed our packs and made our way around to the water below. "These dam paths are too steep," said Steve.

He was right, of course, but it didn't do any dam good complaining.

At the bottom of the trail we met Gordon Bletz, the man on duty at the power station. Because I had had two summers' experience working for a power company I had some idea of what American power workers are like. There was something different about Gordo. I think it may have been the way he wore his hard hat. Or maybe it was his hockey jersey.

Gordo was friendly and enthusiastic about his work. He cheerfully answered all our questions about hydro station operation. "A couple years back," he told us, "a group of canoeists come through and put in too close to the tailrace. Just as they entered the water, Winnipeg opened the gates. Lost all their canoes. Good thing nobody was killed, eh."

Eventually Gordo saw that he couldn't answer all our questions without showing us some of the equipment. Would we like to have a tour? We would.

"But we'll have to go back to the top and get the rest of our gear and the canoe. We'll be right back," we said.

During the quarter hour we had spent with Gordo, something evil had happened.

The wind, which of course had been blowing steadily all day, had gusted up and had whipped the canoe off the bank, placing it right in front of the dam. By the time we were within sight of the boat it was only 10 yards offshore but was picking up speed as it rushed toward the concrete wall.

Immediately, Steve threw off his shirt and ran to the water.

Somewhere before the edge he ejected his shoes and before I knew it was swimming after our runaway craft.

I, too, had reacted quickly. Before Steve was sucked even halfway toward the dam, I had snapped a good three pictures of him and the canoe. "He'll appreciate these someday," I thought.

From my vantage point it was obvious that the empty canoe, driven by the wind as well as the current, was winning the race. I called out, and Steve returned to shore. Together we watched our boat blow away from us.

Suddenly we were struck with an idea. If we got our fishing poles, maybe we could hook the boat with some of the big fishing tackle we had packed. Quickly, we ran to our gear and loaded our rods with our biggest tackle. Steve drew his pole back and, with a deft cast, placed a treble hook securely on the lifejacket we had tied to the seat. With a little careful reeling of the line, the boat was soon safe again. Next time we'd tie it.

We returned to Gordo and took the tour he had promised us. We had never seen so much dam machinery in one place. Steve had changed clothes and was now listening intently to an in-depth explanation of gearing ratios, flow rates and energy generation. I think he especially appreciated the part about how each turbine inlet is shielded by a large protective screen. "Does anything ever get through?" he asked.

"Maybe," laughed Gordo, "but by the time it does it's chopped up so well that you really couldn't tell what it was."

We laughed too.

As we carried the canoe over the rough boulders that made up the dam's exit, setting the boat into the bubbling waters just beyond, we were glad that we had met Gordo. We were glad for the time we had shared, for the chance to have become acquainted with him and especially for the fact that he had turned on the flood gate override switch.

Carefully, we navigated our way through the narrow channel and, braving several rows of standing waves, found ourselves once again in the main river. Another dam portage behind us, we thought. It wouldn't be the last. But it was the last dam portage of the day, and for the time being that was enough.

We swung the canoe to the west and started out. Greeting us cheerily was our old friend. If we hadn't known better, we would have thought it was another dam headwind.

# CHAPTER TEN

# The Mountie's Daughters

*Some people say that there is no romance
in India. Those people are wrong. Our
lives hold quite as much romance as is good
for us. Sometimes more.*

**Rudyard Kipling**

We knew we were almost there when we saw our first cows.

Over the past 10 miles the land had gradually flattened, and the thick woods had smoothed into the rolling farmland that now surrounded us. Weathered and falling fences extended a few feet into the water to hold the herds that grazed on the green fields. A rotting sod-covered shack completed this picture of prairie life.

It would be silly to say that we were afraid of the cows. They were perfectly harmless, we knew. But this was Canada, and we were in a canoe. So, when a large group of the animals decided to rush to the shore to inspect the strange craft passing so close to their domain, we felt that it might be better to stick to the middle of the river. Steve, standing in the bow to get a picture, almost took a soaking from that decision.

We had been working our way down the Winnipeg River for

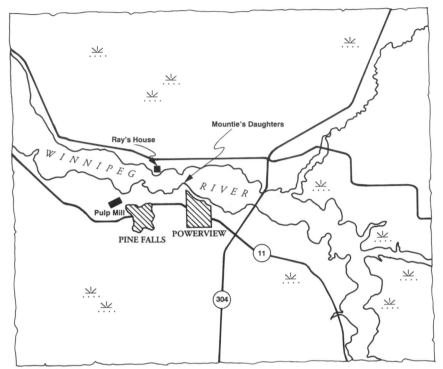

*A riverside herd of cows provided a hint of domesticity.*

almost a week, struggling each mile against the fierce wind that threatened to carry us back home. At the widening of the river called Lac du Bonnet (Lake of the Hat) we had been forced to don our own bonnets in a driving hail storm and take refuge on land for the better part of a day until the winds died down.

We had grown impatient during the waiting. And even now, as we glided easily by our bovine observers, our thoughts spun around an unarticulated question that hung in the air. We had expected an easy drift down the current of the Winnipeg River. "If we were stranded for a day here on the river," we thought, "how long would we be stuck on the lake itself?"

"Weeks," Ray Hutchison would tell us later. "You could be windbound on that lake for weeks and never have the chance to touch the water. The groups that paddled from here in the last century used to carry enough supplies for three weeks. The trip across shouldn't have taken more than one, but those guys knew better."

Ray, too, knew better. An employee of the Abitibi-Price Paper Company for most of his 50 years, Ray ran the Pine Falls water station on one side of the river and had his house on the other. Neither was more than six miles from Lake Winnipeg. Nothing, it seemed, could pass along that river without Ray knowing about it. We were perfect examples.

After paddling past the farmland of the upper delta, we had left the cows and taken our last dam portage of the trip. In fact, the Pine Falls portage was the last portage for three hundred miles. Now all we had to do was paddle. If the wind would give us the chance.

We had planned on stopping at Pine Falls anyway to stock up on supplies. Because we wouldn't have to be carrying overland for awhile, we planned to splurge on fresh fruit and such.

We stopped alongside a family that was fishing from the shore and asked where we might find a grocery.

"We're not from here," one of the older men explained, "but I think that there is a store up over that hill."

We thanked the man and stepped from the boat. "I used to be a baker," he continued, walking with us. "Worked nights for 47 years, well, 'till '85. Never got near the water."

Our conversation was interrupted by the sound of an outboard. Speeding toward us from the far side of the river was a stocky man. His green Hawaiian sport shirt was hanging loosely around the disheveled khaki shorts at his waist. On his feet, one of which was propped up against a brace of his aluminum fishing boat, were rubber thongs. It was Ray Hutchison. As Ray approached, he seemed particularly fascinated by our canoe and gear. People had often stared, and Ray was no exception. Maybe it was our precision-loading technique. "Tossing in the stuff," we called it. Or maybe it was something else that caught Ray's eye. Whatever the case, we took an instant liking to the man—even before he invited us over to camp on his point.

After we had explained a little about our trip he gave us directions to a nearby store.

Later, pulling up to Ray's dock, we secured the canoe and

scampered up the rocky hill leading to the house. As we moved we noted the diving platform on the rock wall overhanging the river. When Ray had been growing up he and his classmates had often sneaked over to this spot with their sweethearts to swim and dive. After he acquired the land he made the board as a tribute to those days.

The Hutchisons already had guests. Ray's wife, Nesta Hutchinson, met us at the door of the screened-in porch and introduced us to Ray's brother Pete, their friend Joe and Joe's wife, Betty. They were drawing on some cold Canadian beer and welcomed us cheerily. Ray was out back cooking up some of his famous marinated pork chops. We had stumbled upon a dinner party. We could live with that.

Before dinner, during dinner and long into the night, we heard story after story of the north woods, Lake Winnipeg and life on the river. Each person had a tale to tell and we listened intently, filled by the chops and eager to pick up information about the lake we were about to face.

Life on the lake had changed a great deal over the past 50 years. Pete, born in Pine Falls in 1927, had seen most of it. The trip to Norway House, he told us, used to take five days on the old wood-fired freighter the S.S. Kenora. It had been a real voyage, with stops at every port to pick up wood to keep the vessel's fires alive. With the coming of diesel, he noted somewhat sadly, the trip had been shortened to two and a half days.

Ironically, technology was the lifeblood of their small community. Pine Falls was a company town and it relied upon its industry for survival.

Over the years the workers had become tightly knit. And they worked hard. Extremely efficient production was their reward.

Actually, the real name of the company town was Powerview. Pine Falls was simply a separate community of people trying to break free of the company. As we saw it, the main difference was that in Pine Falls you could decide yourself when you wanted to cut your own lawn.

The Pine Falls plant specialized in newsprint. During peak periods, production reached eight boxcars of paper per day.

The wood for the mill came from the millions of acres of forests surrounding Lake Winnipeg. Each winter, three-person crews were contracted by the company to head into the bush. Over winter roads through the frozen swamplands, they would haul out the thousands of cords of timber needed at the mill. The wood was then taken to designated points on the Winnipeg shores and stacked to be ready for the spring thaw. As soon as the ice moved off the lake, barges left Pine Falls to pick up the waiting logs. The plant, working at full capacity, could go through a 600-cord barge load in a single day.

In the past, timber had been floated down the river to the plant. As supplies along the river grew scarce, this practice was discontinued. This presented problems for the mill. In the early days, the logs had arrived with little or no bark. Soaking in the water, the covering had become soft and most of it was torn off on the way over the nearby dam. The river bottom beneath the dam is still covered with several feet of bark and old buried logs.

The benefit of this bark removal was a cleaner raw product. Modern printing presses, we learned, use a thin sheet of paper. If the sheet broke during a run, it could mean a great deal of expense to the printer. To make superior paper the Pine Falls mill required a clean log for its pulp.

The barge transport system forced a change in log handling at the plant. When the barge arrives at the plant it is unloaded with a bulldozer. The logs are simply pushed overboard and left to soften. The person operating the retrieval machinery has a crucial job. Not only does the operator have to pick up the logs, trying to knock off as much bark as possible, but also has to do so without driving off the edge of the barge. "But the water is only about 40 feet deep," remarked Ray, "so it's never really a problem finding the machine."

During the winter the water takes on a different significance. The river itself becomes a road. After a deep freeze makes the river passable for a light vehicle, a pickup equipped with a post hole digger is driven onto the ice. At various places the truck stops and plunges its helical blade through the ice and into the water below. Flashing silver as it pumps the cold water onto the frozen surface to thicken it further, the turning blade has an interesting effect on the mariah, a strange eel-like fish common to Lake Winnipeg that lives deep within the chill waters.

Attracted to the glimmering metal, the mariah swims toward the light. As they curiously near the blade they are caught up in the suction and whisked onto the ice above. Over the years, the sea birds of the area have learned this well. During the winter they can be seen following the post hole digger—waiting for a free meal.

When the ice has been made safely thick, the first brave truck drivers venture across the road in their rigs. They always travel with open doors. Who could blame them?

Conversation turned toward the land around us—the woods, the hunting and the past. "We used to hunt moose up here every year," said Ray. "Even after they'd left home, my brothers would come back and we'd head out. You know, you just can't really find out how a guy has been until you're sittin' down at a campfire. Can't really talk. When you do get to, you realize that deep down you haven't changed that much at all."

Ray had switched from beer to whiskey. He poured himself another slug.

"But I'll tell you one thing, eh. Hunting's changed. In the old days we'd ski a full day back into the bush before we set up camp. When you shot a moose then, you'd gut the thing, quarter it and free up the rib cage, cover it with water and let it freeze. Made the perfect toboggan for hauling out the meat. Now they've all got snowmachines. Just tie the thing onto the back and you've got it out in an hour. Doesn't seem right."

We dozed in comfort that night in the protection of the cool screen porch. For generations voyageurs and traders had camped on this point and slept. Wrapped tightly in our sleeping bags, we thought back on the past and the stories we had heard. We dreamed that we, too, were forging our way into a new and exciting wilderness. Looking back on it, I guess we were.

When we finally left Pine Falls we proudly wore our new Royal Canadian Mounted Police baseball caps. They were dark blue with the brilliant insignia of the corps blazed on the front, and we hoped that we might use the caps to avoid any trouble up ahead. "Mountie cadets," we would say, quickly flashing our Manitoba fishing licences. "Do you have a permit for that gun?"

Sgt. Dave Sparrow, a Mountie at Powerview and a relative of Ray's, had given us the hats. We had met Dave across the river.

With him he had his fearless Mountie dog Flash. Still a puppy, Flash already showed the traits that would make him invaluable in the bush. We hadn't seen these traits, but, being inexperienced, we had accepted the Mountie's word for it. Apparently it is a good sign that when called the puppy looks up, yawns and plops down on the ground.

Sgt. Sparrow had two daughters. Cathy was 23. Laurie was 22. Both were visiting from British Columbia. Wanting to discuss the various economic and political changes that had been taking place in B.C., we had decided to spend some time with them.

Later, as we pushed out into the current, we waved to the people gathered at the water's edge and made our way toward the lake, hats tightly secured against the gusty wind. Paddling past the barges unloading at the mill, we glanced beneath us at the cloudy water. Ray had told us of the millions of gallons of chemicals that were poured into the river. With the normal river flow of 35,000 cubic feet per minute, the dilution was rapid. At the present flow of 8,000 cubic feet per minute, we had to be more careful. We'd wait awhile before taking that first drink, we thought.

As we made our way toward the lake we could feel the intensity of the winds. Before we had paddled five miles we had two inches of water in the canoe from the chop. Though not unusual for us, it was somewhat annoying. This time it was particularly so because my camera had been sitting on the bottom of the boat. As we caught our first sight of the great lake I reached for the camera to get a picture. I took it from its case and yellow liquid ran from behind its back. The water and its chemicals had got to the film. Frustrated, I put the camera up on a pack, wondering if the blues and greens had been ruined as well.

We made about eight miles our first day on Lake Winnipeg. Ray had said that we'd make 15 if we were lucky. I guess we weren't. Our one satisfaction was that we did make Mitas Point, the traditional jumping-off place for those heading up the lake. It offered the last natural protection before the lake opened up, and it seemed a good spot to wait out the wind. The point was sandy and warm.

It was a perfect place to lay out our sleeping bags. I closed my eyes. I dozed. I dreamed.

"A Mountie always gets his man, Scott." With great effort I tried to shut out the vision. There in my dream, decked out in full Mountie uniform was Dave Sparrow. I tried to run, but it felt as if my legs were bound together. All I could do was barrel roll. Finally, he caught me at the edge of a large waterfall. With lightning speed he grabbed me in a giant fist and hurtled me off the edge, far into the spray below.

Burrowing deep into my mummy sack I tried to ignore the water . . . but the rain was seeping into my bag and I had to do something.

Steve had the same problem. We burst from our cocoons and dashed for our boat and the tent it held. We set up the shelter, threw in the bags and crashed inside.

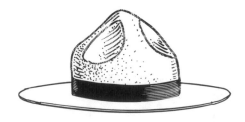

# CHAPTER ELEVEN

# Ghosts

*"Paddle! Paddle! The rocks!"*

**Walter Port**
**From** *Canoeing with the Cree*

By morning, the fury of the night had given way to stillness.

The unruffled lake took on a strange beauty, its many islands seeming to float over the shallow waters. "We'll be off the lake in no time," we thought. Quickly, we loaded up the boat, pushed it off its sandy berth and headed out into the vastness of the lake.

After an hour we saw Devil's Island on the horizon. In the past, Indians and non-Indians alike had stopped on its rocky shores to make offerings to the gods and devils of the lake, thanking or hoping for safe passage. We passed up the opportunity. That might have been a mistake.

When we turned on to Lake Winnipeg, the scale of our maps had changed. We no longer had the detailed 1:50,000 maps that had guided us this far. Instead, we used the larger and more general 1:250,000 scale. Though good enough for the big lake, the new scale had a curious effect on us.

For more than a month we had stared at those folded green papers. They had been our guides, and we had marked our progress by the inches we covered and the number of maps we could retire

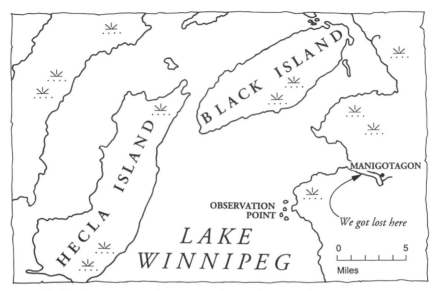

*On all of Lake Winnipeg there was only one place to take a wrong turn.*

in a day or in a week. Now it took five times as long to cover the same amount of distance on the paper. Navigating from the stern, I often folded the map so that it could be read from where I stuck it under a pack strap. That way I could follow our progress as we moved steadily along the page. Now things had changed and it was hard to gain perspective. We seemed to crawl along. Boredom overcame us.

Once, to break up the routine, I impulsively launched my paddle high overhead in the direction of Steve. I couldn't explain it then and I can't explain it now. But it seemed to help. Steve retrieved the paddle. I stared at the page.

On into the day we paddled, trying to occupy our minds and make the time pass. The points seemed so close on the map, but hours passed before we would reach the landmarks.

Late in the afternoon we approached a long reef. It was a mixture of small islands and hidden dangers and extended out into the lake farther than a mile. In the calm waters we glided easily among the rocks. Finally landing at a large flat tablerock, we stopped to cook supper. While we waited for the water to boil over our small camp stove Steve took a look at the map. "Hey," he cried, "this must be Observation Point!"

He pointed out our position on the map. I realized that he was right. We were sitting on one of the rocks of the reef where Sevareid and Port had almost lost their lives in a storm so many years ago. Looking around at the smooth, benign waters, it was hard to believe.

The images of Sevareid's book rushed around us. As if hoping to make out the vague outline of Sevareid's and Port's canvas craft, we strained our eyes over the water.

We had come to this place to see the land they had seen, to experience the things they had experienced. Yet our Observation Point was not theirs. What else would be different?

After we had finished our dinner of macaroni and cheese we left our rock and pushed up the lake. The conditions were favorable, so we didn't want to waste time. Though the sun was setting we pushed onward, figuring that we could camp on any of the flat islands we had seen. Besides, there really wasn't any danger of getting lost on Lake Winnipeg—not even at night.

I still blame it on the larger scale map. Steve, however, holds that it shouldn't be possible to paddle five miles up a river thinking the whole time that you were circling an island. In the end, the sound of the Manigotagan waterfalls gave it away. On all of Lake Winnipeg there was only one place where you could take a wrong turn. We had taken it.

An hour and a half later we had worked our way out of the river and back onto the lake. Once there we found a relatively flat rock and threw out our sleeping bags to wait for morning. The bugs thanked us for the gifts of our bodies.

With morning came the sight of whitecaps. Undaunted and eager to leave our sleeping bags, we loaded the canoe and pushed off into the seas. Before we had paddled more than a mile we were forced to flee the open water. Somehow we managed to guide our fragile craft over the breaking waters and between the numerous threatening boulders that studded the otherwise sandy shores.

Dumped on the beach, we struggled to pull the canoe away from the water. Soaked, we stared at each other, not quite sure what to do or what to make of the situation. When the rain started we reached for the tent.

Normally it's a simple operation, but erecting the tent on the windblown beach was a major feat that day. No sooner would we have the nylon firmly fastened to the poles than the wind would grab the structure and either deform it or send it whisking down the beach with us scrambling after it. The stakes we had driven into the sand barely slowed the tent's flight.

After perhaps half an hour of effort we finally had built a camp that we were fairly confident would last long enough for us to get inside. The canoe, filled with packs, sat as a monolithic wind block on the windward side. Every available piece of rope and tarp was lashed to the structure in an attempt to make it secure. The broken sticks scattered about the place made our camp look like the site of an 18th-century shipwreck.

Lake Winnipeg was different from Lake Superior in several ways. Though a good deal smaller than Superior, and much shallower by hundreds of feet, Winnipeg in even a light breeze would blow up whitecaps in a matter of just a few minutes.

Refuge was easier to find on Winnipeg than on Superior, though. When the storms did blow, the shores of Winnipeg offered many bays and easy landing places. Provided, of course, that we could make it to shore.

Another distinctly pleasant difference was water temperature. Unlike frigid Lake Superior, Winnipeg in mid-summer was warm and made for a pleasant swim. As we waited out the blow we aimed to take advantage of that feature. Having just barely survived our first Winnipeg test we did the only sane thing left to us. We stripped off our clothes and hurled ourselves into the billowing seas.

# CHAPTER TWELVE

# False Dawn

*She walks in beauty, like the night,*
*Of cloudless climes and starry skies,*
*And all that's best of dark and bright,*
*Meet in her aspect and her eyes.*
*Thus mellowed to that tender light,*
*Which heaven to gaudy day denies.*

**George, Lord Byron**

The winds died enough the next day for an early morning departure.

Hugging the shore, we were able to paddle the half mile to the end of the point that had been giving us some protection against the northerly wind. When we tried to round the point we were met head-on by the stiff wind. Defeated before we had begun, we turned the boat and landed on the lee side of the point.

Sunning ourselves in the protection of its mass, we found it hard to believe that just around the point four-foot waves were pounding the shore.

The wait certainly could have been worse. In fact, since that day there have been many times when I have wished for a day of such complete leisure, sitting in the sun on a sand beach with absolutely nothing to do.

But at the time we had other ideas of enjoyment. We were anxious

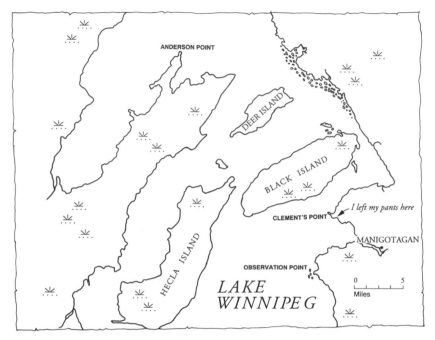

*The canoeists were still short of the narrows—and already beaten.*

and wanted to get moving, no matter how pleasant the circumstances. When the lake reached up onto the beach and grabbed one of the sneakers I had left there to dry my resentment of the wind only grew. My mom had bought me the shoes and, ugly as they were with their multicolored random stripes, they were the only shoes I had. Now I would have only my boots.

Probably the worst part of the situation was that, deep down, we knew that it could get worse. It probably *would* get worse.

Lake Winnipeg is shaped much like an hour glass. When the northern winds blew the fury was broken up at the narrows, and the water backed up in the southern end, creating the famous Winnipeg wind tides.

As we sat impatiently on our point we knew we were somewhere below that neck in the most protected spot on the lake. We were beaten already, and we hadn't even got a glimpse of what the open lake could dish out.

As we bided our time at the beach we organized and dried our gear in the sun. As I sorted through my stuff I realized that my trail pants were missing. "I must have left them back at our other camp," I thought. Not willing to put the canoe back in the water, I made my way along the shore. When the heavy brush made progress difficult, I took to wading in the shallow water. The water was murky from algae and I couldn't see exactly where I was placing my feet. If I had been in a movie, something unseen would have grabbed me with fish-like hands and dragged my struggling body below the surface. I assured myself that it wasn't a movie and continued on.

Suddenly the lagoon around me exploded. Water splashed everywhere, and I could see loathsome forms sliding beneath the water. I couldn't move.

When I finally regained my senses, I realized that I was perched on a nearby boulder, Buck knife in hand. A dozen and a half good-sized carp circled in the water below. I spent the better part of the afternoon searching for the monster that had tried to attack me, but all I found were my pants and the carp. After some thought I decided not to frighten Steve with the story.

As darkness came on we tried once more to round the point. Though the waves were down it was still too risky. Back on land we tried to catch some sleep. Not wanting to unpack the canoe to get the tent, we tried again to sleep in just our bags. During the day we had lazed about bug-free. Now they were back. Disgusted, we jumped up, threw the gear into the canoe and pushed off. We'd round that point or die trying.

Luckily our patience had lasted just as long as the wind. This time when we came across the point we encountered only one-foot waves—a size we could easily handle. After another hour of paddling, the waves were gone entirely and we found ourselves the only movement on the water.

Navigating wouldn't be a problem. If we just kept heading to the west around Clement's Point we couldn't go wrong. And with the silver of the moon in the sky, the night wasn't so terribly black. There were no rivers to mistakenly paddle into. Only open water. And the night chill.

As we continued on into the night that chill became greater—like the deepening cold of an October morning at home during hunting season. But there were no ducks here, and no warmth of the coffee from a dented metal thermos. At first our excitement at being underway had overcome the cold. Then the weariness hit. But the memory of Clement's Point pushed us on. And in the darkness we couldn't have stopped had we wanted to.

After several hours we rounded Black Island and were on the far east edge of the lake. Soon we were deep within the thousands of islands that lined the eastern shore. Here, immersed in the silence of the night, the world took on an entirely new look. It seemed as if we had never been anywhere else or done anything different. Searching the horizon intently for the first glimmer of sun, I thought back on the past and tried to recall details. I could not.

A glow appeared and life began to become real again. The surreal fog around us was lit briefly and our spirits rose. But it was not the true beginning of the day we had awaited. A false dawn.

By the time we made it to the end of the archipelago it was light enough to pitch a tent. We had learned our lesson about the bugs. At this point sleep couldn't be sacrificed to speed and, though the day promised to be clear, we set up the tent and jumped inside. When we awoke several hours later we had a southerly breeze, an unheard of gift in that part of the world at that time of year. With it, we anticipated making short work of this lake. Ironically, it almost meant the end of us.

# CHAPTER THIRTEEN

# Horror at the Fish Camp

*Of all the things I've lost,*
*I'm going to miss my mind the most.*

**Anon.**

The steady tailwind was too tempting for people so naturally lazy.

After paddling around a gull-covered island that virtually exploded with life as we passed, we made land and began the construction of a high-tech wind catcher. While Steve went into the woods to cut some saplings, I set on a pot of Red River Cereal goulash. We had heard that Canadian children eat a bowl every day before school, so we brought two pounds for the trip. I must admit that it is an ideal wilderness food. One small bag lasted the whole trip. But what we didn't eat we could use to anchor the sail.

The best sail for a canoe is a two-poled V. Two corners of a tarp are secured to the ends of poles. The free ends of the tarp are rested on the bottom of the boat in front of the bow seat. The person in the bow then holds the loose end of the tarp with his or her feet and spreads the upper end to catch the wind. Provided the wind is blowing in exactly the right direction, this setup works very well.

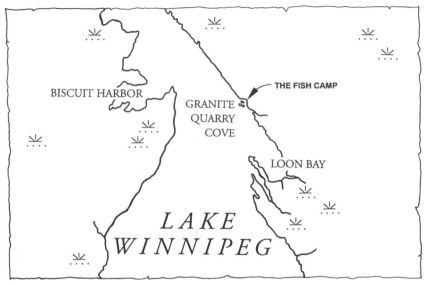

*Active minds and idle hours led to fish camp fantasies.*

The obvious problem is a disconcerting lack of visibility. The person in the bow sees only tarp. The person in the stern, with considerable straining, can see obstacles in the water only provided they are extremely large and not in the path of the canoe.

But if our sail worked, we'd be at Berens River for the Fourth. We were willing to risk it.

As we scooted along the water we soon learned that we could, with proper positioning, move at almost the same velocity as the waves—most of which were a good three feet high. To avoid rocks we maintained a fair distance from shore. Sitting in the back, I struggled to keep the boat properly aligned.

When struggling to paddle into the wind it is natural to dream of sitting lazily in a canoe with a sail up. At such times I always imagine myself kind of kicked back in the stern, leaning against the gunwales—opening my eyes only occasionally to give the steering oar a quick twist. Panic is rarely a part of that picture.

We were panicking now. Intoxicated at first by our new-found speed, we had decided to cut across a five-mile bay that extended deep inland toward the southwest. Even if we could have paddled the bay it would have added at least 15 miles to our distance without giving us any real protection. So we cut across.

As we eyed the far shore, we noticed that the wind seemed to be increasing. Occasionally, a rogue wave ran past the canoe and broke over the gunwale. Other waves, catching us from behind, would lift the stern and try to wrench us broadside. Furiously, I leaned on my paddle to gain control and straighten the boat.

By the time we were halfway across the water we were out of control. Had we had the cover on I think we would have fared pretty well. But to accommodate the sail's poles we had removed the splash cover. In these seas it would have been impossible to put the cover on without losing the boat. We were taking waves over the sides. I looked down at my feet. They were covered with water. We were sinking.

Our first thought was to drop the sail so both of us could paddle. But even if we could have taken down the sail, our situation would only have worsened. We still couldn't have put on the cover, and without the extra speed of the sail we would never make it to land. Realizing this, Steve propped the poles with his knees and began digging his paddle into the water. We might make it.

In our rush to land we almost forgot to keep our limited lookout. Steve, struggling behind the raised tarp, could see almost nothing. I wasn't much better off.

When we were about a mile offshore Steve stopped paddling long enough to reach around the tarp and peer ahead. "My God!" he cried, "we're going to hit the reef!"

Shocked, I swung the boat to left to see what he meant. In an instant I knew. The shore ahead was safety, if we could make it that far. But between us and refuge, not more than 200 yards ahead, lay a virtual wall of submerged rocks. Inside the rocks was a bay. From the spray being thrown into the air I knew the rocks weren't far beneath the surface. Our frail craft would be dashed to pieces on them.

I still don't exactly understand what happened in the next few minutes. For weeks afterward I would swear that I had seen an island in the middle of the waters and had swerved the canoe to slip into its protection. But there was no island, and when I turned I saw only water. Water and the dangerous reefs we somehow had passed.

Once past the horrible rocks and within the protection of the small bay, I felt that I could breathe again. I looked back and saw how lucky we had been. That water was no place for a canoe. Steve was the first to speak. "Good thing nobody died, eh."

With the relief of safety came the ability to survey our surroundings. We landed the canoe and explored our new-found home.

Apparently we weren't the first to have appreciated the natural shelter this harbor afforded. Though labeled Granite Quarry Cove on the map the place looked more like an abandoned fishing camp to us. On top of a low hill, set deep into the tall grass and weeds, were the remains of a half dozen cabins. We moved closer.

One of the buildings, sagging and decrepit, housed the remains of dozens of gill nets. In the dim light that passed through the holes in the walls the nets looked like huge eerie spider webs. In another building we found rusting pieces of machinery and old outboard motor parts. Scattered about were the meat tins we were to see everywhere.

More recent activity was evident in a shack in the center of the clearing. The shack was the only building that appeared to have a sound roof. The building was enhanced on the inside by sheets of plastic that had been draped over the walls and ceiling. Leaning on the wall was an old Hudson Bay ax, its handle scarred and darkly stained. Its blade had remained strangely sharp and rust-free.

The Winnipeg Free Press lying on the old barrel stove was from August 1985. The headline had been circled with a bold red marker:

### FAMED AXE MURDERER THWARTS
### POLICE, ESCAPES INTO BUSH

Finding nothing of particular interest, we left the room and stepped again into the bright sunshine.

Our curiosity satisfied for the moment, we took stock of our situation. Put simply, we were stuck. The density of the woods and brush around us precluded serious exploration. The surging water blocked us in that direction. Until the winds felt ready to let us depart we were as good as prisoners on this small jut of land. But unless something unexpectedly evil happened, we should be OK.

We decided to set up camp on the flat spot overlooking the lake.

From there we had a good view of the entire point and we thought the wind would keep the bugs away. We *did* have a good view. As the sun set we had no trouble at all seeing the bugs as they descended on the tent. It was great fun watching the blood-thirsty insects land on the doors and windows as they tried in vain to find their way in. It would have been more fun, however, had we been inside at the time. As it was, a great many of our friends joined us before we could frantically close the doors.

When we had finally murdered the last one of them, we spoke quietly. "It shouldn't be bad hanging out here for awhile," mused Steve. "It'll sort of be like a vacation."

I broke in. "We're getting out of here tomorrow."

By the third day I knew we were losing it. It was July 5. On the morning of the Fourth Steve had said he was going out to chop some wood. Busy drawing an American flag on our instant cheesecake with strawberry squeeze jelly, at first I thought nothing of it. But we had broken our ax weeks before.

Later that day we sang *America the Beautiful* to the strum of the guitar and danced around the camp stove in the tradition of our hometown. Earlier we had killed some time by trying unsuccessfully to nab carp in the nets we had found. We found that they worked better on the seaweed.

Then Steve decided to shave his beard. Raising his body from the pool of water in which he had been working, he turned to show me his handiwork. With the beard gone and his face slashed unrecognizably from what had passed as his razor, he looked like a white devil. I began to worry about him.

After the first day we had read all the old *Newsweeks* that Ray had given us in case we got stranded. The second day we read the ads. By the third day we were reading the parts of the magazine that no one should be forced to read. We knew who published it, who edited it, who the chief researcher was. It was not that we didn't have other things to do. When we didn't want to read anymore we could always go down to the canoe and sort and count the food. Of course, sleeping was always an option, as was sorting through the food. Did I mention that?

We were beginning to learn French. On each box of Canadian pancake mix we found our lessons. It was the perfect time for a perfect family breakfast. *L'ideal pour un parfait petit dejeuner en familie.*

Clever, the Canadians. In America we would have been eating plain old pancakes, although in most parts of America they wouldn't have been like ours—charred and an inch thick.

But in Canada we feasted on *melange a crepes complet Au Babeure* Aunt Jemima. They tasted the same, but we felt better about them.

Inevitably, though, we returned to the *Newsweeks.*

When, on the evening of the fifth we started feeling sorry for the mosquitoes that had been clinging to our tents I knew we had better get off soon. We wanted to get a picture of them. So I had offered my arm as a lure. They couldn't even fly enough to get on. "How heroic," we thought as we gently replaced the door so as not to hurt them. We were in trouble.

That night I went back to the center cabin. I thought that I might pick out some of the old papers and read the comics or something. Closing the door firmly behind me, to keep out the howling wind, I entered the dark chamber. I lit the candle that sat atop the old warped wooden table and picked up the newspaper that was next to the candle. In the dim flicker of the flame I made out the words on the front page.

Apparently a psycho killer had escaped from the mental hospital in Winnipeg. Once a baker, he had worked nights for most of his life, filling his days with comic-book horror fantasies. As his condition deteriorated, he began making his fantasies come to life.

He committed his atrocities not impulsively but only after studying his victims over a period of time. Mondays, it said, had always been his day off, and that's when his victims got it.

There was more, but the candle began to die. In a rush I searched through the rest of the papers. Unfortunately somebody had already taken all the funnies. That was too bad, because I knew how much Steve always enjoyed them. Disappointed, I blew out the guttering candle and returned to the tent.

When I awoke the next morning it occurred to me how different this Monday was from other Mondays in my life. Usually Monday meant the end of something pleasant—a weekend or a brief holiday. Today, the fact that it was Monday didn't mean a thing.

As I pondered this thought I became aware of a strange stillness. The wind was down. "Hey," I yelled, "it's gone! The wind's down! We can leave!"

"But it's Monday," replied Steve sleepily, "I don't have to work today."

We were a hundred feet offshore before Steve spoke again. Somehow we had packed the gear and thrown it into the long-useless canoe. It had been a tough wait, those days at the camp, but it was over. We were free again, and safe from whatever ghost might be there.

CHAPTER FOURTEEN

# The Melting Pot

*The first large commercial use of aluminum was in cookware.*
*Aluminum cookware heats up quickly and evenly.*

**World Book Encyclopedia**

We paddled 50 miles on that first day of freedom.

For the voyageurs, it would have been a 16-pipe day. That was how they had measured their distances. After each hour of paddling they had been allowed a five-minute break—and a smoke of the pipe. Figuring four miles an hour, we would have had 16 pipes. We had our pipes, but we didn't stop.

Along the shore we saw two black bears, a refreshing sign of life. Around midday we reached the neck of Lake Winnipeg, the Winnipeg Narrows. The water there is only a couple of miles across and offers about the only reasonable spot for crossing in a canoe.

In the afternoon we stopped to eat some lunch. Having forgone breakfast in our rush to leave camp, we were hungry after a 20-mile paddle. We stopped first at a small island not more than 30 yards from shore. Not a wave could be seen. But through our fear, the wind still had its grip on us. "Don't you think we better go to the mainland?" asked Steve. "If the wind picks up we could be stranded here." We moved.

We had spaghetti for lunch. When we finished our meal we hit

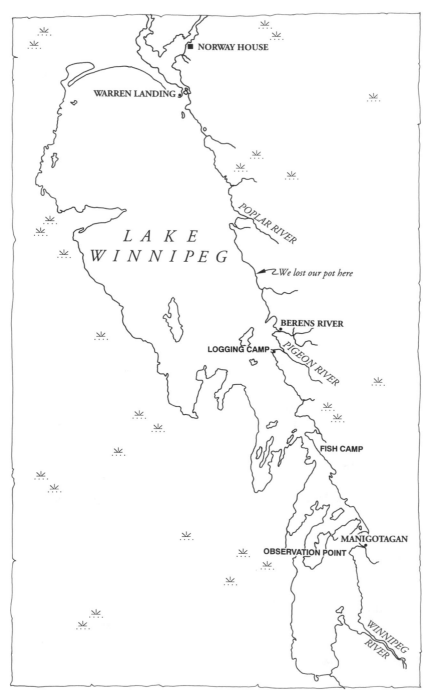

*The lake held many points well taken.*

the water once more. We had hoped to make Berens River by the Fourth. It was already the sixth and we aimed to make it that day.

As we made our way over the still water it was hard to believe that the same languid lake had almost crushed us just days before. Now this same water merely quenched our thirst.

When we had first entered the lake we had been overjoyed to be finally rid of the fishflies in our drinking water. Closer examination, however, had revealed that the water itself was not all that appealing. From a distance the water was light green, and it was tainted throughout by a distasteful algae. As our canoe passed through the floating scum, it cleared a path through the algae and left an interesting pattern trailing off into the distance.

Before we left Duluth we had been told repeatedly to boil our water to kill off the Giardia parasites. For the first few days after Grand Portage we had been diligent. At the end of a hard portage, though, it is hard to wait for the water to boil. Soon we were relying on handkerchief filters. After that, whenever troubled by stomach pain, it became common practice to count back the gestation period of Giardia—10 days. "When did we camp by that swamp? Wasn't that about 10 days ago?"

The green water of Lake Winnipeg called for more than handkerchiefs. Calling on his chemistry training, Steve whipped up an algae filtration system consisting of a handkerchief, a plastic wide-mouth bottle and gravel and sand of various sizes.

Holding the cloth over the mouth of the bottle, he would fill the cloth, starting with sand and working his way up to the gravel on top. Then he would pour the lake water into the filter and let it trickle down into the bottle.

Steve claimed that the filter worked well, but I always wished that he had cleaned the sand first. At any rate, I think his professors would have been proud.

In the hours after lunch we consumed a lot of water. We paddled steadily, without stopping, without talking.

There was one thing that I always thought strange about such times. When, after hours of endless tedium, the silence was finally broken, the words were almost always simple statements of obvious facts.

"Can't believe how thick that brush is," we'd say. Or, "It looks like the wind is picking up."

You'd think that after all those hours of contemplation we'd come up with profound philosophical contributions to the thinking world. We didn't. With time, it got worse.

The cruel fact was that, for the most part, our minds were occupied with thoughts of food. Steve thought of donuts. I of burgers.

Two hours down the lake we did get in a nice meal. It was just getting dark when we approached Pigeon Point, the last extension of land before Pigeon Bay. Another five miles away, just across that bay, stood the Berens River settlement.

If we hadn't noticed the man standing at the shore we probably would have reached Berens River that night. At least we would have made it across the bay. But we did see the man standing there. He looked small against the hundreds of logs piled around him. He was the first person we had seen in seven days.

We pulled the boat toward his silhouette. His name was Kelly. He worked for the mill loading lumber onto the barges that hauled it down to Pine Falls. We asked him if the barges ever had any trouble with the wind.

"Well," he replied, "this is how it works. You see tugs pull an empty barge up here from Pine Falls and exchange it for a loaded one. The trip takes about 24 hours, and they run night and day. Sometimes the wind comes up pretty fast—guess you guys know that, eh. A few times the tug has lost a barge in the wind. When the load tips it makes trouble on the lake. Six hundred cords of dead-heads can make a mess for the fishermen."

Kelly eyed the sun setting over the canoe. "Say, come on over to the other side of the point," he invited. "We've got camp set up there. Maybe Marie can get you something to eat."

Marie, the cook for the small lumber loading station, got us more than just a little something to eat. She loaded our plates up with so much bread, bacon and cheese that we slumbered deeply through the night and late into the next morning.

Wearied from the hard paddle the day before, we dozed right through the sound of the growing wind that was whipping up the waters of the bay that separated us from our next destination of Berens River.

By the time we managed to drag our bodies from the sleeping bags we could see that we would have to hurry if we were to beat the waters that day. Pushing our covered craft out behind the protected side of the island on which we had camped, we shouted our thanks once more to the loggers for their hospitality and the mosquito coils they had given us.

It was a good thing that we didn't try to traverse the bay that day. In our enthusiasm to reach the settlement that was producing the smoke we could see on the other side of the water, we started to make a direct line for the opposite shore. When the first wave broke over the side of the boat and washed right over the light nylon spray cover, we thought better of it. So, seeing that it would be hopeless to try to reverse our course and wait it out on the island, we ran with the wind and tried to make the end of the bay. There at least we could find shelter in the mouth of the Berens River.

As we approached the end of the bay it was apparent that the lake once again had the better of us. By that time the waves were a good five feet high and were carrying our craft like a surfboard. Struggling desperately to keep the canoe in line with the wind, we managed to push the boat into the mouth of the river. We cursed the wind, the water and our own impatience for wanting to get across.

We spent that night on a spit of sand at the river's mouth, not even a mile from where we had started. To the north lay the Berens River settlement. It was just five miles by water and a mere two or three over the land. But it might just as well have been a hundred. It would have been futile to try to hack our way through the dense and swampy spruce growth that surrounded us, and we couldn't have launched the canoe again even if we had been crazy enough to attempt it. There was nothing to do but pull out the pipes and wait—once again—trying to look thoughtful and just a little bit bemused.

Over the years the pipes had become our secret weapons. Dreading the thought of actually having to smoke them, we nevertheless carried them on every major outdoor adventure—just to have them along in case the need arose. They helped our fishing, our hunting and, most important, our storytelling. Without a pipe it was just a story about a five-pound walleye. With a pipe it was a tale of great daring, adventure and expertise. Nobody could question the facts. Nobody would dare. "Now I don't profess to be an expert on walleye. I would, however, like to say this . . . ."

The next day the wind went down enough to allow us to move on. We hurried up the shore and around the point. Sevareid and Port had stopped here for several days. We were eager to get our first look at the Cree settlement.

A great deal can change in 50 years, particularly if those 50 happen to be in the middle of the 20th century.

As we arrived we were struck by the strange lack of boats running about the river. Occasionally we would see the long wooden skiff of a fisherman. The skiffs were always white, and, with their long protruding bows and powerful outboards, they were the ideal fishing boat for the lake. But they were few.

Later we were told that pickup trucks and sedans, brought up by ferry from Winnipeg or driven over the frozen winter roads, had replaced the boats. No permanent roads had yet reached the settlement from outside.

The village at Berens River had a grocery. The Snack and a Half—a Canadian ice cream sandwich—cost 60 cents. It was our first chance at such food since we had left the comforts of Pine Falls eight days earlier, and we happily munched down two each as we hiked along the dirt road to the post office a mile or so up the river. We debated whether we should paddle there. But our legs, weary from the long sit, decided that the hike would be good. At the post office we hoped to find mail from home.

Later that day, after a successful mail run, we loaded the canoe with a five-pound bag of flour and four pounds of spaghetti. The price, we noticed, was considerably higher than at the southern end, where stores were more accessible.

On our way back to the canoe, we stopped at the bright red Coast Guard cutter Nomad. The ship cruised the big lake, repairing buoys and marking dangerous reefs. At harbors the crew often placed two large targets to identify a safe passage. Boats could keep the two markers in line and thus stay in the safe channel.

Eager for any advice we could get about the lake that lay ahead of us, we called up to the bearded man on the deck.

"Looks OK right now," he replied, "but there isn't much for shelter between here and Warren's Landing. And the north winds can really blow. Stick close to shore."

We felt a little nervous as we pulled our boat away from the protection of Berens River that afternoon. Nearly 60 years earlier our predecessors had stared out at this water helplessly as they watched the unending northern wind strand them at the settlement. They had been forced to ride a freighter the remaining 150 miles up to Norway House and had skipped the northern shore of the lake entirely. From here until Warren's Landing, we were entirely on our own. If we got caught in the wind we would be truly stuck. There would be no freighters.

Several days later we felt once again the strength of the lake. We also lost our first pot.

Lounging on a beautiful sand beach the morning after a hard paddle, we decided to wait out a westerly chop. The shoreline for the last 60 miles had been an uninterrupted strip of white sand a good 15 yards wide, sloping gently up to the scrub and stunted spruce that lined the eastern shore of Lake Winnipeg. These trees, woven so tightly together as to all but prevent passage, grew to only six or seven feet tall.

The trees and the white beach created a strange, confusing illusion. From four or five miles away, the trees appeared to float several feet above the horizon—silent, beckoning mirages. The effect was particularly eerie during the still periods when nothing could be heard but the rhythmic stroke of the paddles.

To pass the time that day we experimented with baking bread. Applying all our knowledge of science and engineering, we first dug a deep pit in the sand. We filled the pit with load after load of the driftwood we found scattered about the beach. Steve stoked the ensuing blaze while I prepared the dough.

Ever since we had left Duluth we had carried a vial of yeast. Wanting to ensure a good sized loaf, I dumped the entire contents of this vial into a bowl and mixed it with water that Steve had procured by swimming out into the lake and away from the scum-covered water on the shore. A little sugar and a lot of flour later we had a goo that we considered the beginnings of bread.

This mess I then spread out on our breadboard-paddle and went to work. By the time the fire was ready I had finished kneading the dough.

Then, following a procedure we had seen once in a Mark Trail camping tips book, we placed the risen bread ball into the smaller of our two pots, which we then enclosed in a larger pot covered by a plate. Thus secured, our little oven was buried deep in the glowing coals of the fire. We waited for the success of our endeavors with a swim in the waves.

I guess Mark Trail hadn't used aluminum nesting kettles. In any case, we shouldn't have. When, in great expectation, we uncovered our device, our big pot was gone—melted and lost forever to the driftwood fire. The bread wasn't in much better condition. Charred an even black on the outside, our bread ball remained doughy and cool on the inside. We cracked it like a coconut and found that it would hold water.

By the time we had cleaned up the mess and properly mourned the loss of our pot, the wind had gone down just enough to allow our departure.

On a large-scale map the northeastern shore of Lake Winnipeg appears almost as a straight line. In reality, it is composed of long curved sections broken by gentle points. While the jagged reefs of the south had given way to beautiful sand beaches, any wind at all could easily kick up waves too big for a canoe to handle. We never really got used to that fact, and it always seemed strange that in the midst of tremendous breakers the water beneath us might be only three or four feet deep.

Such was the case that day. Cutting once again from point to point, we paddled the covered canoe quickly to the north. Strangely, the wind switched unexpectedly and picked up speed from the southwest. Realizing that in the covered canoe we could ride out nearly any wave from that direction, we continued in ill-founded confidence.

Minutes later we were a quarter mile offshore in swells of at least eight feet. At that point we decided that fun was fun but that we weren't in control any longer. We weren't really even paddling. Instead, we were "catching" wave after wave and riding them until the next one picked us up.

Given this predicament, Steve took the next logical step. Pulling his camera out from under the protective cover, he turned around and snapped a picture of me. In the seconds that it took to complete this, without Steve's paddle controlling the front, the canoe swung precariously to the left and a wave washed over our breached canoe. Steve dropped the camera onto his lap and we brought the boat back into position. I breathed again. The picture is nice, but a bit out of focus.

When the wind switched to the west we were forced to yield. Remembering the Coast Guard officer's warning, we looked to the barren and bayless shore. It presented nothing but boulders. Slowly, we pushed onward, realizing both that we could not land the canoe with the crashing waves and that we could not continue. We were reminded of our first day on Lake Superior. That was all it took.

Heeding the deepening water in the boat—its sloshing was threatening our stability—we decided to make a run for the shore. Picking out what looked like a relatively smooth section of sand, we turned the canoe and raced headlong toward the shore. Because of the crashing of the waves, we couldn't see the boulders standing in our way. So, blindly, we paddled a straight line, miraculously avoiding the rocks. Even so, we came in so fast that we were dumped on the beach with a crash. We were stunned by the force of the landing, and it took several seconds to react and haul the boat and gear out of the way of the other rollers. Safely ashore we holed up again and waited it out.

Our last day on the lake actually was a night. It was several days after our last big adventure and we had been inching our way up the unpopulated coast—paddling when we could, waiting when we had to.

On July 12 we stopped just before Muckawa Bay and ate some spaghetti and rice pudding. Without even unpacking we waited for evening, hoping that we could leave with the still of the setting sun. Even the beauty of the place could not ease the restlessness of our souls. Our eagerness to get off the lake grew with each hour that we were stranded. We just wanted off.

As we had hoped, the wind let up just before the sun went down, and we slid off into the dark waters. At first we paddled in silence as we worked our way around the islands that were now popping out of the previously barren shore. Then we began to sing. One song led to another as we ran through our entire repertoire. Sometimes we knew the words—we added our own where we did not.

With a reddened moon as our only companion we threaded our way through the broken islands, the only sounds disturbing the stillness were our hoarse voices and the occasional crunch of Kevlar on an unnoticed reef. We were the only people in the world, a world that hadn't changed in a thousand years.

We reached Warren's Landing at about noon the next day after a five-mile open-lake crossing. Waiting there at a sagging and weather-worn dock were two old men speaking to each other in Cree. We pulled the canoe up to them and shouted a greeting through the wind and asked about Norway House.

The man who answered was wearing a blue baseball hat, a faded wool shirt and jeans. Sticking out in tufts from the rubbers on his feet were rabbit-lined moose moccasins. He answered our inquiry in an accent somehow combining Scotch, Norwegian and English but in a purely Cree style we would learn to appreciate. "Norway House," he replied, "OK, lots of people—that's for sure, eh?"

We were exhausted from our long paddle and asked about islands for camping. We were told of a number of good spots. The men were staying at the bunkhouses near Warren Landing, once the landing spot for all supply boats of the Hudson Bay Company, now a refrigeration site for fish taken from the lake.

The bunkhouses, like most of the structures at the landing, looked rundown to the point of uselessness. "How are they in the rain?" we asked.

"Oh, no problem," the man said.

"Don't they leak?"

"Not as long as it doesn't rain."

Satisfied, we paddled on our way—safe from the lake at last, a mere 15 miles from Norway House. Four hours—no more.

# CHAPTER FIFTEEN

# New in Town

*Here I belong, but the green weeks fly.*
*And Autumn's brown fingers are painting the glen.*
*Answer me wild geese arrowing high,*
*How can I live in the town again?*

**Irene Stanley**

I was confident.

"Can you believe that those guys got lost in here? All you have to do is follow the eastern shore straight up around Niaposkitayosik Point and then up the channel to Norway House. How hard can that be?"

We were sitting on an island just at the beginning of Playgreen Lake, the island-infested body of water between Lake Winnipeg and Norway House on the Nelson River. Sevareid and Port had been told that the name came from "plague-of-a-lake" because of the difficulty of navigating through the maze. In fact, the two had themselves become lost in a cold wind and rain.

But it was sunny on our day there and calm, and we had the advantage of a modern map to guide our every turn. We would be at Norway House in time for lunch.

After four hours of paddling we realized that something was wrong. We sat in a maze of islands, none of them on our map, all of them covered with hundreds of white pelicans. We threw insults

*Thanks to uncharted islands, the canoeists got extra paddling practice.*

at the mapmaker and debated where we might be. After detailed study of the chart we guessed that what we had followed as the shore on our right actually had been a tightly packed group of islands. These had been guiding us not to the north but gradually to the northwest. Given this, we decided that if we headed straight north we would reach the entrance to the channel leading to the settlement.

We paddled on until Steve spotted a navigation buoy in the distance. Although it looked as if it marked a solid piece of land, we traveled the mile or so to the red float and saw the land split. The beginning of a channel. Relieved, we moved into the opening and headed north. Several hours later we knew we were really lost. What was worse was that we could not imagine where we had gone wrong. For four or five miles we had been following a wide channel curving to the northeast. But none of the shapes or islands matched the channel we thought we were following.

Thoroughly confused, we welcomed the small white house we saw in the distance as a chance to get our bearings.

As we approached the site our concentration was interrupted by a dive-bombing gull intent on driving us away from her chick, which was swimming in front of us.

When the barrage ceased we looked up and saw the white steeple of a church and a forestry lookout tower looming in the distance. Consulting the map we realized the truth.

In front of us was Rossville and to our right the famous Hudson Bay post of Norway House. We had missed the channel entirely but had found the settlement in spite of ourselves.

Norway House had for centuries been a key post in northern Canada. As a supply point and depot for the Hudson Bay Company, it had quickly developed into an important hub for commerce in this remote territory. Here furs and goods were exchanged between the Orkneymen who hauled the furs northward through the Hayes River to York Factory and the boats working their way southward through Lake Winnipeg and into Selkirk and eventually down the Red River. Before the development of American rail transportation, this route had been the most economical means of transporting furs and goods through North America. Eventually, evolving economic realities ended the trade.

Unlike the voyageurs of the North West Company, the Hudson Bay Company traders had relied on the larger York Boat for their transportation. The traders could use the York Boats—complete with a sail for Lake Winnipeg—because they faced fewer and easier portages.

Rossville was the Indian counterpart to Norway House. When the Hudson Bay Company had first established the post there was no permanent Indian settlement of any kind along the shores of the

Nelson River. With the coming of the company, however, a group of Indians began to live just across the channel from the fort. Uncomfortable with a settlement so close to the depot, the Factor of Norway House had cleared the land at a site several miles away on the other side of Norway House, declaring it a settlement and enticing the Indians to move there. It was that settlement that we now saw from the water.

On a point of land between Norway House and Rossville we spotted the flag of the Royal Canadian Mounted Police. We headed in that direction to check in and get what information we could.

That evening we paddled down the channel to Playgreen Inn. The Mounties had directed us to this spot. We had read of it in Sevareid's account.

Fueled with a meal cooked by someone else, we left the inn in darkness. We hoped to find a camping spot on one of the islands the Mounties had pointed out.

"Any of those islands is OK," the Mounties had said, "but you probably shouldn't go over to Rossville—they don't take too kindly to strangers over there sometimes."

The first thing we noticed at Rossville the next morning was the church. Sitting on a grassy point out from the rest of the settlement, it was the most picturesque church we had ever seen. It was a one-room wooden structure, painted white with green trim, and it looked as if it had been there forever. As we pulled the canoe onto the shore in front of the church we saw that the asphalt shingles were being replaced and the whole church was being redone. We walked past the church and into the settlement, eyeing the workers curiously as they replaced the old shingles.

As we returned to the canoe that evening we were struck once more by the church. This time we stopped and called up to the roof. "You guys need any help?"

"Inside—the floor!" was the reply.

We opened the heavy pine door of the church and looked at the dark woodwork and the hardwood floor. It looked a hundred years old—worn dark by successive coats of varnish and the dirt from decades of footsteps.

In one corner stood two electric sanding machines along a patch where someone had started the tedious job of removing layers of dirt and varnish. Steve and I looked at each other and then each of us grabbed a machine and got to work.

About the time the sun was setting, the workers on the roof were finishing and climbing down their makeshift ladders. One of them, a young man in his early twenties, wearing paint-splattered jeans and an old black T-shirt, popped his head in the door to see how we were doing. He watched for several minutes without speaking, probably trying to find just the right words. He did. "You guys new in town?"

# CHAPTER SIXTEEN

# A House of God

*But seek ye first
the Kingdom of God,
and His righteousness,
And all these things
shall be added unto you.*

**Matthew 6:33**

The days we spent working on the church were some of the best of the whole trip.

While we waited for the arrival of Steve's brother Mike and our friend Bill Kubiski we went to the church first out of curiosity and then to help.

For the first few days we camped at an island a mile or so offshore. From there we would paddle to Rossville and work all day with the Indians.

One day for a diversion we wandered over to the forestry office at Norway House. There we met Kay Allen. Her husband, Denny Allen, for 27 years was the forestry director of northern Manitoba. They lived at Forestry Island. It was the lookout tower there that we had seen on our arrival at Norway House. Over a cup of coffee generously sweetened with condensed milk, Kay invited us over to their island that night. We eagerly accepted.

Denny Allen—tall and lank—was exactly what we expected. His

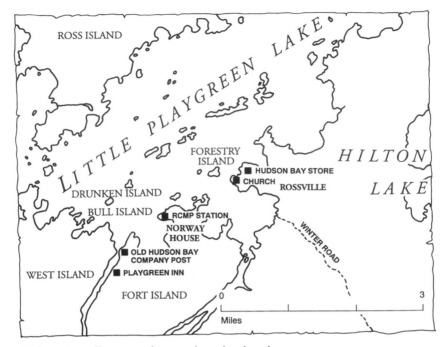

*Life at Rossville centered on work at the church.*

weather-worn face showed every year that he had spent in the bush. He also had the peculiar conversational trait that we had become accustomed to in the North—the long silence. Steve and I, so used to the activity of school and city life, had grown up with animated conversation.

With Denny, as with so many of those we had met, pauses in conversation were not at all uncommon. At first we would wonder if the people had forgotten about our existence altogether. Then they would say something, and we would realize that they were, well, just thinking. We learned to wait.

Denny had seen a lot in his years at Norway House. Only five years ago had the dirt road from Winnipeg come to the community. Before that, the only contact with the outside was the weekly freighter up the lake, and that only in the summer.

In the winter a covered sleigh had carried the children to school. Hot bricks kept them warm until they arrived at the one-room schoolhouse. In the summer they had taken the canoe.

Forestry Island had once housed as many as 30 people—foresters, Mounties and the like. Later we saw pictures of the first float plane to land at the island. That was in 1911.

We learned that we were camped on Drunken Island. The York Boat crew members, returning to Norway House after six weeks in the woods, had been ready to live it up. Rather than put up with the destruction of property that this was sure to cause, the Factor at Norway House had sent all the returning men to this island for a couple of days. With them he sent kegs of rum.

Given this, we weren't surprised to find that the island was covered with the old clay pipes of the adventurers. The pipes had been dispensed by the company and were sold already filled with tobacco. They were perhaps the New World's first disposable consumer good.

The neighboring island had an interesting history as well. Years ago a bull that was kept within the walls of the Norway House Depot had become enraged and had gored a young clerk to death. In retaliation, the Factor ordered that the bull be taken to a nearby island, covered with tar and set afire. Since that day the island has been known as Bull Island.

The pastor of the small church was a Cree named John Crate. Pastor Crate had one set of clothes, a Bible and all the love in the world for the people of Rossville. He walked everywhere he went, wandering the community, tending to those who needed his help. One day Pastor Crate explained to us that he himself had rented the two powerful sanding machines from Winnipeg. The church had only enough money to keep them another week. Because everyone was so busy working on the roof he hadn't thought that they would be able to finish the inside. Then, unexpectedly, two outsiders had paddled up in a canoe, offering to help.

But our rewards were greater than our efforts. After several days of work, the chief of the band, Allan Ross, came to talk to us. Rossville had been named for his grandfather. In his loafers and cardigan sweater, Chief Ross looked more like an accountant than an Indian chief.

Introductions, we found, were unnecessary. The chief knew who we were and what we were doing. Best yet, not only did he have his own cherished copy of *Canoeing with the Cree*, he was actually the son of two people Sevareid had met during his time at Norway House—Ralph Bouchardt, a Hudson Bay Company clerk, and Mary Ross, a Scottish woman at the settlement. Both were mentioned in Sevareid's account.

Chief Ross had learned of the work we had done on the church and wanted to thank us. When he turned to go, he shot us a quick smile. "Say," he asked, "how would you boys like to come stay up at my house while you're here?" Would we ever!

The next day we packed up our gear and left the camp at Drunken Island. Back at Chief Ross's home we were greeted by half a dozen children who were eager to help carry our packs and canoe.

Life with the Cree was filled with work at the church. We would sneak off occasionally to the Hudson Bay Store for a Snack and a Half. As much as anything, we were fascinated by the way the price varied from fifty cents to a dollar fifty depending upon the judgment of the person working the counter.

In the evenings we went swimming with the kids and took them for rides in the canoe. We were surprised that they had never been in a canoe. We had expected to be shown up by their skill but found instead that the outboard motor had replaced the paddle almost exclusively. The one exception was the annual York Boat race during the Norway House York Boat days late in August. The event "celebrated" the treaty that had signed away 100,000 square miles of Cree land in 1864. For this each man, woman and child was to receive five dollars each year "for as long as the grass would grow."

The Cree children had little adult supervision and would stay out with us long into the dark. Around midnight we would make them go home so we could get some sleep. This independence had developed an impressive camaraderie among the children. Not once while we were there did we hear one kid make fun of another. Instead they shared everything and supported each other in a way highly unusual among the children we knew.

For example, when we first met 12-year-old Marcel, his speech difficulty was explained to us by the other kids before we even noticed it. "Marcel's OK," Andrew explained, "he was born that way."

The kids had built their own "Tarzan swing" on which they

proudly displayed their prowess for their visitors. They had two other favorite sports. The first was "bucking bronco." Steve and I were the broncos. After awhile we found we were no match for the tireless boys.

More of a concern to us was their game of playing shipwreck with our canoe. When we weren't around they would find the canoe, fill it with 10 or so of them, and begin rocking it side to side on the grass as if in a storm. Then they would shipwreck, hit a reef and all tumble out. Once Steve went up to the house and found them using the overturned boat as a steeplechase obstacle. A few blood-curdling shouts later and they were on their way.

We were surprised by the number of blonde Indians we met. In fact few of the Indians we met were full-blooded Cree. They were a mixture of Cree, Scottish and English. This combination was also responsible for the accent we often heard. Invariably each sentence would end with a rising tone. In the word "canoe," the "ca" was hit hard and the "noo" trailed off a good two steps higher in pitch.

One day young Robert came to us with a burning question. "Mr. Scott," he asked, "may I see your mops?"

"We don't have any mops."

"But I've seen 'em. They're in your ca-noo."

"No, we just have those sponges."

Irritated, Robert walked over to the canoe and grabbed a roll of our maps. Very strange.

Most people at Norway House still spoke Cree to one degree or other, but it was only the older people who conversed in it daily, speaking little English. The most Cree we heard was on the local radio station which, when not playing old Hank Williams music, made local announcements in the monotonic Cree.

The Cree people did not develop a written form of their language. Pictographs—paintings made on cliffs near the water—served as the only form of written communication. Often these were painted while the artist stood in a canoe, inspired as often as not by the legendary fun loving spirits—the *May May Kweesiwuk*.

Denny Allen had cataloged hundreds of pictographs for the park service.

When the Methodist missionary James Evans arrived to minister to the Cree in 1843, he built the first church on a knoll overlooking the water. He also developed what is known as the Cree syllabic, a written language that phonetically describes each sound of the language.

A language reflects the depth of a culture. From what we learned of Cree this is certainly true. Descriptive in a way strange to English, Cree had over the years adapted itself to the new ways of the Europeans.

Timekeeping as we know it was an unknown concept to the Cree before the coming of the new people. The Cree culture focuses on the purpose of each element of nature. Thus their word for clock, *Peesim Okan*, translates literally as "man made sun."

Technology carries with it its own ideology. Cars, outboard motors and VCR machines cannot be had without adopting at least a certain amount of the culture that begat them. This was evident everywhere. Plastic littered the roads. The bright white, green and red bags of the Hudson Bay store cluttered the water's edge.

Once we followed the kids down to their favorite swimming spot. Andrew, having just finished the last of a pop given to him by Robert, tossed the can into the water. Steve couldn't believe what he had seen, and asked why he had done it. "I was finished," Andrew replied. The concept of littering was strange to him even when faced with the ultra-realistic fact that he now had to swim where he had just dumped the garbage.

Chief Ross told us that the greatest problem in the area had come when the family system of work was upset. Previously nomadic trappers who went into the settlement for only a few weeks a year, the Cree families had been broken apart with the coming of mandatory schooling and other white ways.

Success in Cree life had called for a family to work as a team; the father and older boys ran the trap line, and the mother cleaned the furs and prepared the meals. When this way of life was eroded away and was not replaced with any real alternative, the people grew more and more reliant upon government aid.

For a time the church had been the focus of youth activity in the settlement. The churches were the Cree's first schools and provided after-class activities, too, and fostered a feeling of belonging through outings and choir. With the introduction of government schools (whose accommodations rivaled the largest schools in the States) these church groups died away.

Services at the church were in the afternoon. No specific time was set; they simply took place. Originally services had been half in English and half in Cree, and the United Church of Canada had a special Cree-English hymnal. During that time part of the congregation had sung in Cree, the other in English. But because the monotone nature of their language had caused those singing in Cree to drag through the music slowly, the pastor realized that the two languages were simply not compatible. Now the services are conducted in Cree.

During our time at Norway House we made a significant addition to our trail menu. We had long heard about bannock, the historic food of the Hudson Bay Company, and through the help of Denny Allen and several Indian women we perfected our preparation of the dish.

Sevareid wrote that bannock would "ruin a white man's stomach in two years, if he isn't careful," but we found the frying-pan bread to be a wonderful trail food. Its name stems from the Latin word *pannicum* (communion bread). Bannock was brought to Canada by Scottish traders of the Hudson Bay Company. It consisted of any sort of flour mixed with baking soda, grease and water. It was cooked over a low fire.

We were given any number of recipes for the bread but the one we generally followed was given to us scribbled on the back of a fur trapper's declaration form. It was:

*2 cups flour*
*2 tablespoons baking powder*
*2 teaspoons sugar*
*2 cups water*
*some lard*

Denny Allen said that his usual recipe was three flour, two baking powder, four sugar, two lard and three water. Because we were never quite sure which units, if any, he was using, we left his recipe alone.

Actually, we learned that the recipe isn't nearly as important as the fire. The first several times we made the bread it was black on the outside and gooey on the inside. After awhile we learned that the secret, after mixing the ingredients and dividing the kneaded dough into two parts, is to squash the pieces as flat as possible and cook them high above a very low fire. We had been cooking them like pancakes and were having no success.

All during our stay with our Cree hosts, we continued our work on the church. One night, after putting down our tools, we looked out over the lake and saw a tremendous thunderstorm heading in our direction. Soon the rain engulfed us. But we were warm and dry in the old church, and we sat at the open windows watching the storm.

Several days later we returned to the newly sanded floor to find it tracked with the muddy footprints of a small child and a large dog. We groaned and set to mopping up the mess before putting on the varnish. This time we nailed the door shut as we left.

By the 23rd the floor was finished and ready for the pews to be moved back in. Two days later Steve and I stood in front of the beautiful church. Beside us were Chief Ross, Pastor Crate and our two canoeing partners, who had just joined us for the trip to York Factory. Together we made one last inspection of that house of God before setting off into the water. Satisfied, we closed the heavy wooden door behind us.

# CHAPTER SEVENTEEN

# The Solitude of Four

*A foolish consistency is the*
*hobgoblin of little minds.*

Ralph Waldo Emerson

I don't profess to be an expert on canoeing.

I would, however, like to say this: It is impossible to live on the trail with another person, each day traveling as far and as fast as possible, without developing a particular and often peculiar wilderness system—a way that these two people have of doing day-to-day chores that creates as little friction as is humanly possible. Such a system is simple, and decisions require minimal, if any, discussion. In fact, life itself requires only a minimal amount of discussion. Meals are made, tents are set and dishes are done.

During our two months in the woods Steve and I had achieved such a system, and things generally went smoothly—due as much to a growing apathy as to a concern for each other's welfare.

But when we left Norway House on the morning of July 27, our system was threatened by the age-old challenge to travelers: new guys. As we waved a final goodbye to Pastor Crate and the others gathered by the cool green shore, we wondered how it would be paddling with our new companions the remaining difficult miles.

Keeping our thoughts to ourselves, we turned quickly around the first bend of the Nelson.

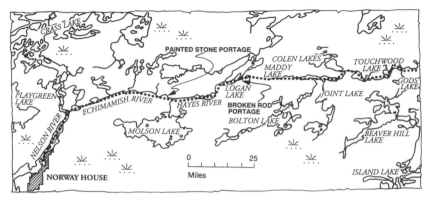

*On at least one map—this one—Maddy has a lake named for her.*

Our new traveling partners, Steve's brother Mike and "Kub," as Bill Kubiski was known to us, had a red canoe. That's how we could tell ourselves apart.

They also had jobs and could grow nicer beards than we could. Mike even had a baby girl back home.

Mike and Kub, too, had waited a long time for the big trip. We had paddled with them many times in the past on short fishing trips and they had dreamed with us of the big trip.

Because of their other commitments they couldn't take the whole summer off. Instead, they relied on a brand new pickup truck, a driver who was gracious enough to make a grueling round trip, and a thousand miles of gravel road, which ended at about the spot that we reached after two months of paddling.

Because of their differences, and because they hadn't had the benefit of our two-month transition period, the attitude of the paddlers in the red canoe was strikingly different than ours.

They had come to fish and believed in stopping for lunch. Somewhere between Duluth and Norway House, Steve and I had lost sight of our need to stop during the day. Most probably this resulted from our tremendous fear of getting stuck on Lake Superior or Lake Winnipeg.

We were, however, willing to adjust and didn't mind stopping for the occasional handful of gorp or candy that the other pair had brought. It is important to be flexible in the bush.

The first part of the the remainder of our trip would be a piece of cake. Having approximately 500 miles to cover before we would reach York Factory, we would paddle along the Nelson River and then turn east onto the Echimamish, cross over the Hayes system and end up on Gods River, which we would follow to the ocean.

From Norway House the Nelson River is a straight shot into Hudson Bay. But because of its immensity and high-volume intensity (it carries the combined flows of the Red, Saskatchewan and Winnipeg Rivers—draining a basin as far west as British Columbia) the route was not used by the Hudson Bay Company. Instead, the York Boats were hauled over to the Hayes. This route was possible because of the canal-like channel of the Echimamish.

Five miles down the Nelson we gained an appreciation for the river's power. Hearing a roar in the distance, we scanned the river and saw the first major rapids of the trip. We pulled the boats up to an island that parted the river and took a quick look at the situation. Following a dropoff of five feet, the river poured through a trough with speed enough to crush our canoes and scatter our gear. A portage it would be.

Once the gear was safely on the other side, however, we hiked up to the top again and decided that the passage was safe for human negotiation. At Kub's insistence we jumped into the smooth flow and slid down the shoot. In a matter of seconds our tumbled bodies, buoyed by the lifejackets, were past the falls and far down the river. Steve and I decided that Kub and Mike were going to fit in just fine.

At dinner that night we learned a disturbing fact. Kub didn't "particularly like" macaroni and cheese. Apart from the obviously stunning effect of such an announcement, Steve and I were faced with the additional problem that half of our food packs were loaded with the stuff. Maybe if we called it something else.

A day later we turned off the mighty Nelson and began working our way up the Echimamish. This small passage, lined closely on both sides with dense scrub spruce and willows, takes its name from the Cree word meaning "the river that flows two ways." This curious fact made possible the Hayes River route used by the Hudson Bay Company traders. They had followed the Echimamish all the way to the headwaters of the Hayes, just yards from the end of the river.

Ironically it was the beavers that contributed a great deal to the success of this route. By damming the flow many times over its 50-mile course, the animals slowed the current and ensured water deep enough for passage of the large York Boats. With the extermination of the beaver in the area—they were nearly trapped and hunted out of existence earlier in this century—the company had to install its own waterworks, the remains of which we saw at several locations.

Judging by the number of their dams we had to cross, the beaver had made quite a comeback in the years since the decline of the fur trade. At first we were dismayed by the obstacles. After clearing a few of the dams—usually masses of interwoven sticks and trees rising one to two feet above the water—we began to adopt the correct system. Once we spotted a dam, we gave the signal: "Ramming speed."

With that we would paddle as fast as possible, trying both to achieve maximum speed and to plane the boat as high as possible in the water. If all went well, our efforts resulted in forcing the bow of the canoe up and over the edge of the dam. Then Steve would step out onto the branches and pull the canoe along just enough to let me out. Once we were both back in the canoe, we would teeter-totter toward the bow and I would free the craft with a push. Later we learned that this was the same procedure followed by the crews of the York Boats.

By that time the once smooth finish on our Kevlar hull had been worn, scratched and repaired until it looked like a patchwork quilt. A beaver dam or two made little difference. For Mike and Kub, though, every twig hurt. The beautiful red finish on their canoe was still unblemished. We could see them wince with every scrape.

On the 29th of July, we reached the headwaters of the Hayes and pushed our way over the smooth rock that separated us from the next watershed. On the other side we found Robinson Lake, the first real lake we had encountered since Norway House. Along the Echimamish we had come to wide spots in the water that were labeled on the map as lakes. Each time, however—as with the appropriately named Hairy Lake—we found them to be actually nothing more than shallow pools, clogged completely with thick growths of rush. Paddling was unpleasant but not impossible.

At Robinson Lake we took the opportunity to refresh ourselves in the open water. It was also a treat to be able to paddle in a straight line for a considerable distance. While the Echimamish covers some 50 miles, its straight-line course is less than half that. This means, of course, that the river meanders back and forth. In addition to adding extra miles to the trip, it was particularly frustrating that for most of one day we were not able to take more than four strokes at a time without making at least a 90-degree bend. In a smaller river canoe this would not have been such a problem. But our Odyssey was eighteen and a half feet long and was made for the waters of big lakes and didn't like to turn. We hoped that it would learn by the time we reached the rapids of Gods River.

From Robinson Lake it was a relatively easy paddle to Robinson Portage, a one-mile carry around some rapids to Logan Lake. Muddy and wet from rains the day before, the portage was nevertheless clear of brush. All along the trail was evidence of the fur trading past. Though not mechanized to any great degree, the portage had at one time been made at least more passable with the introduction of a light rail over which goods and boats had been hauled. The source of power, however, remained the human body.

In no hurry, and noting the condition of the path, we opted to make the portage in two carries—first bringing over the packs and then going back for the canoes. Upon our return, however, we could not resist the temptation to try our hand at the rapids in our empty canoe. The voyageurs would have called this a *demi charg*, too dangerous to run with gear but just tempting enough to run with empty boats. But, of course, the voyageurs had never been here. Mike and Steve agreed to carry the remaining gear with them to the bottom of the rapids and Kub and I set off in the covered Odyssey.

By the time we made it through the rapids to the pool beneath the falls, it was growing cold and dark. Mike and Steve had already left the rocky landing in search of a campsite.

After paddling a quarter of a mile or so through thick reeds, Kub and I finally pushed out into the open lake and searched the dimming shore for signs of the others. Not seeing the canoe or any signs of a fire, we quietly analyzed the situation. Steve and Mike had both tents and all the camping and sleeping gear. That could be a problem, particularly with rain on the horizon. We, on the other hand, had the food. If worse came to worse, they would have to find us.

Minutes later the orange of a fire glowed from the southern shore, and our shouts broke through the cry of the loons and the rush of the wind. We headed for the light and found Steve and Mike working hurriedly to find a place to pitch the tents before the rain.

I think we would all just as soon forget the next section of the trip. Until we left Logan Lake our course had been pretty much laid out, and the portages, though difficult, at least existed. For the next 60 miles, as we attempted to cross the watershed of the Hayes and get into the Gods system, we would have to find our own way, threading our canoes though a patchwork of sloughs, creeks and swamps.

The night we had first turned off the Nelson, we had set up camp on a small island in the middle of the flow. Cleared and arranged in the fashion of an Indian camp, it was a stopping place for the infrequent groups that traveled to or from Norway House.

Just as the coals of the fire were burning down to an even glow, we heard the rumble of an old outboard. Minutes later four young Indian men pulled their beaten aluminum boat onto the shore. "You the guys workin' on the church?" they called. Apparently communication doesn't always require telephone lines.

We answered, saying that we were now on our way to Hudson Bay.

"Over the Hayes, eh?"

"No, we're going to head over to the Gods."

At this the men shook their heads. One mumbled something in Cree. They all laughed.

And then silence. "Well, we better get going."

As they pushed their boat onto the still waters of the river, one had turned to us and said, "You better be careful through the stretch onto the Gods. Nobody goes that way now. Better take the Hayes. There aren't any portages. Every once in awhile you might find one—but they're all overgrown. Hasn't been used for a long time." More silence.

"Hey, Charles, how long since anybody's gone to the Gods?"

"Figure, hmmmm . . . maybe 30 years."

But at that point the warnings were too late. Dismayed by the report, we took comfort at least in the fact that as Sevareid had said "the residents of each region are prone to exaggerate the dangers of their particular piece of the river or country." Unfortunately, this time there was no exaggeration.

In this land, the lakes had no names. We named them, and those names reflect the feelings and activities that were ours as we crossed the waters with the labor of our sweat. We paddled Biscuit Lake, Crusted Lake and Lostafish Lake. We took Brokenrod Portage and rested along Burned Out Creek. There, amidst the black remains of the forest, we recalled the words of Denny Allen. "There's so much timber up there that if it starts to burn, we just let it go."

The forest service had divided the land into three zones. The green zone was timber that could be reached in the next 20 years. A fire there would be fought. Red zones indicated lands that wouldn't be logged for more than a hundred years. This blackened land around Burned-Out Lake must have been a red zone.

One small lake we found was particularly beautiful. On a cliff along a dark blue shore we saw a date scrawled next to a faded name. *1854.* I guess that back then it would have been considered graffiti. Now it was history. It sent our imaginations soaring.

This lake deserved a special name—and a special namesake. Maddy Lake. Mike's baby girl.

We also named the swamps through which we passed. But to mention those names here is really more than the world is ready to handle.

One of the worst parts about forging through such country is never really knowing what is ahead. Because of the scale of the maps it was impossible to determine what that blue squiggly line on the paper actually meant. The thinnest line on the map could be anything from a stream 10 feet wide to a foot-wide beaver path. The stream could be paddled; the beaver path could not. The beaver path usually holds about three inches of water and has another three feet of muck on its bottom, also making walking almost impossible.

These conditions, of course, make picking a route extremely difficult and progress slow. While a mile of lake might be covered in 15 minutes, the same distance in the swamps would take hours to cross.

Many times the meandering slough ran out completely and we were forced to drag the canoes over the wet ground. Sometimes all four of us would have to grab one canoe to make any progress at all. Often sinking into the slithery mass over our knees, we would struggle to reach dry ground. Then we would begin the tedious process of taking the gear overland to the nearest lake. On such days you learn to love paddling a canoe.

As the traveling got worse, I began to wonder if James Joyce hadn't come through this way at some time during his life:

"Imagine some foul and putrid corpse that has lain rotting and decomposing in the grave, a jelly-like mass of liquid corruption."

How else could he have known—have described it so well? I finally understood him.

One day our luck really ran out. We had been following a trickle of water for several hours when the flow ended abruptly and we were forced to abandon the canoes in search of dry ground. It would have been difficult enough to manage without gear. But with the extra weight of a 70-pound food pack, each step was murder. The biggest struggle was trying to keep out of the mud as we tripped and stumbled over the entanglement of sunken branches.

I choose to keep the memory of that day just a little bit blurred. But I can remember vividly tripping over a sunken root and, being unable to regain my feet, crawling through the swamp on my hands and knees.

Somewhere along the way I lost the others. One moment they were just ahead, each straining under a loaded pack. The next moment they were gone.

Unsure of what else to do, I forced my body to continue to the base of a hill a couple of hundred yards away. From there I dragged myself through the brush and to the top of the hill, hoping to see my friends or the lake ahead.

Exhausted and frustrated, I sat at the top of the hill, unable even to remove my pack. I was so alone. No sound. No life. Just me, my pack and the woods. Sweat continued to run down my face, stinging my eyes. Flies swarmed. I wanted to quit.

In the stillness I remembered the words our old high school football coach, Bill Westholm, used to tell us. "When you cheat yourself," he had said, "you only cheat yourself."

That hadn't made much sense to us at the time, but we had always laughed and tried a little bit harder. It made more sense now. Finally I recovered my breath, grabbed my pack and headed down.

Crashing through the brush, I headed straight east and came eventually to the next lake. Across a small bay I could see a pile of packs. The others had made it. I surveyed the impassable land and, stripping off my jacket, which I had worn for bug protection in spite of the heat, jumped into the water. Maybe I could catch them.

Pulling myself out of the water near the packs, I set off in search of the canoes. Into the woods I ran, breaking through the dense brush. After a short while I came to a small clearing. A clearing? I looked down. Under my feet lay the unmistakable remains of an ancient portage path. Rotting planks lay over the wettest spots of the ground. I groaned. It could have been so easy.

In the distance I heard voices. Seconds later I saw the cheerful faces of Steve, Mike and Kub as they easily carried the canoes and remaining gear along the trail's solid footing. Steve took a long look at my soaked and muddy clothing. "Gee," he asked, "where have you been?"

# CHAPTER EIGHTEEN

# A Burning Sky

*Such sights as these are reserved for those
who will suffer to behold them.*

**Eric Sevareid**

Staring at the fiery glow over our heads, it was clear to us why the people of this lake had named it the Gods.

Sevareid had called it God's Lake, the apostrophe making the name all the more appropriate. For if God were to call one country His own, surely the magnificence of this inland sea would be it.

We spent just two nights on Gods Lake and were twice rewarded with a show of Northern Lights that rivaled anything we had ever seen. For these were Northern Lights as seen in the Far North. They came from all directions and in all colors. To the south we saw yellow and blue shimmerings as they swept up and met the gold straight overhead.

We slept outside on these nights and would wake up in the middle of the night and lie there enchanted. For a time we discussed the lights as a phenomenon of nature, but in the cool air and gentle breeze of the North, we knew that it took more than talk of ions and magnetic fields to describe what we saw. The native people of that land, knowing nothing of our science, had offered a better explanation. It was, after all, God's Lake.

We had crossed into the Gods river system several days before

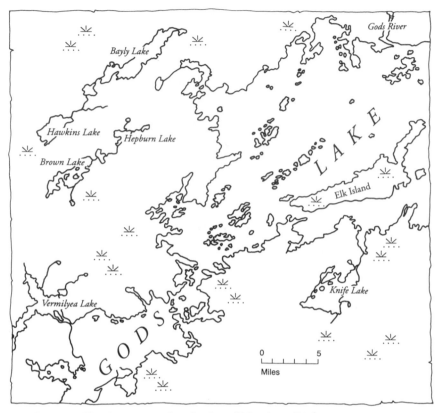

*Gods Lake offered a spectacular display of Northern Lights.*

and, for the third time on the trip, had assured ourselves that the rest would be a piece of cake. This time it had to be true—no more swamps, no more sloughs, just easy lake and downhill river paddling.

At Touchwood Lake we met up once again with our old friend, the wind. But even that couldn't take the edge off our happiness to be back on open water again. We had camped on the lake on a low flat rock island. When we awoke, the wind was washing waves right up to the edge of the tent and we had to scramble to keep the gear dry. It was apparent that the wind didn't intend to let up; so, after playing a few hands of cards for some of our Canadian money, we impatiently put off into the cold waters.

Although we hugged the shore as closely as possible, we could not find protection enough from the onslaught and were forced to wait—cold and wet—on a barren rocky point. Hauling the canoe onto land, we noticed for the first time a gash in the thin sides. No wonder it had leaked so heavily.

The next morning we got up before the wind and rounded the narrows out of Lake Vermillya into Gods Lake. On the rapids just above the great lake, we saw the first people we had seen since a local family had passed us on the Echimamish, two weeks before.

This group, too, was an Indian family. We watched the man at the outboard motor maneuver his 18-foot aluminum fishing boat up the rapids with the skill of a running back. We just looked at each other in amazement that somebody could negotiate that foaming mess without hitting a single rock.

When the boat reached the gravel bar onto which we had pulled the Odyssey, we waved him down and complimented him on his feat. "Oh, it's no problem," he told us, "as long as you don't stop." We wouldn't stop, we thought, but then we wouldn't be running up any rapids either.

It hits you hard when, after weeks of painstaking work hauling a canoe and gear through swamps, up rivers and into waves, you turn the corner onto one of the most beautiful lakes in the North and find a boat loaded with American fishermen. For us, getting here had been an unending battle of endurance; for them it had been a matter of a few hours in a float plane. But perhaps our efforts had changed our perceptions in such a way that we saw a lake even more beautiful, a wilderness more pristine, than those so recently and painlessly delivered here from the outside world. We hoped so.

Later that evening we paddled the canoes past the Gods Lake settlement that Sevareid had made his last kick-off point and pulled up on the shore to wait for the next day—and our big push across the northern expanse of Gods Lake. Sevareid and Port had almost lost their way for good at this point—and in calm weather. We wondered what we could do if the wind kept blowing.

Forgetting our hard-learned lessons of Lake Winnipeg, early the next morning we decided to take advantage of the steady south-westerly breeze. After taking time to stop at an island to cut poplar sail poles, we lashed the two canoes together and struck out. In each boat the guy in front held upright a pole tall enough to fully extend our large tarp.

With a whoosh the wind grabbed the sail as we came out from the lee side of the island. The lightweight canoes creaked as the forces built up. With each gust the thwarts on the Odyssey twisted to unnatural angles. Onward we plunged into the billowing lake. Finally, when one of the rivets popped loose from the front thwart of our canoe, we decided that this sailing thing should be reconsidered. Double sailing was fine for the sturdy aluminum tankers we had used back home in Minnesota, but this wind was just too much for our light, high-tech performance canoes.

By the time we dismantled the apparatus we were well into the open part of the lake. After chucking the poles over the sides we made it to a small island and hastily secured our spray covers. We set off to cover the five miles of open water between us and Green Island. From there we could follow the protection of islands into the mouth of Gods River.

Drawing on our experiences on Lakes Superior and Winnipeg, Steve and I decided to head almost straight northwest so as to meet the southwesterly wind at a good angle. We would then turn 90 degrees, making a straight shot for the island with the wind at our backs. The turn would be tricky, but the swells, though large, were far enough apart to give us a chance.

It took two hours to paddle the distance. After an hour we began losing sight of Mike and Kub. By that time the waves were so large that we could see the red canoe only when we rode up a crest.

It is quite a change of feelings to be riding huge rolling waves in a canoe—fighting desperately to remain afloat and in the right direction—and then to turn a bend and suddenly be in smooth water again. Immediately all cares drain away, and it is hard to imagine what you were experiencing only moments before. When we brought the canoe around into the protection of Green Island, this feeling was ours.

But, minutes later, after we had landed the boat and had clambered up the rocks to get a view of the lake, our relief turned to anxiety. Mike and Kub were still on that water. In a shorter boat, unable to tack into the waves, they had surely been forced to ride parallel to them. We imagined only the worst.

We hoped that they had been driven downwind of Green Island and had been able to continue on to the shore. We entertained this notion for awhile and even considered pushing off ourselves but finally abandoned the idea. As evening was approaching we put up a tent and put together a dinner of macaroni and cheese and fresh raspberries. If that didn't bring them in, nothing would.

Unable to sleep, swim or read, we waited and fished. Actually we just snagged our lines on rocks hidden in the surf, so we stopped and waited again.

Just as the sun was beginning to set, Mike and Kub appeared. Thinking of a child and a wife, and stymied by the rough water, they had waited in the protection of a smaller island to the south, eating berries and fishing. They had seen our fire. They were OK. Again we had survived a scare.

We slept that night on the rocks and saw in the skies the glow of the heavens. Tomorrow would come the river and the end of the wind.

It took us a few crackups before we learned how to handle our big canoe in the rapids. Ever since we had taken the spill on the Maligne in the Quetico we had been cautious about fast water. The first day on the Gods we always stopped the canoe well above the whitewater to scout the best route. We soon learned, however, that if we did this at every rapids we would never make it to the end. So, with growing confidence, we began to simply slow the boat before the rapids stretch, stand up in the canoe to get a quick look ahead and make a shot for it.

For the first several miles of the river we had occasional help from the guides we watched while they skillfully maneuvered their boats up and down the difficult sections. Based at the Gods Lake lodge, they could make it down and back a 30-mile section of the river in one day. We would watch them and try their path. Sometimes it worked, sometimes it didn't.

A technique we learned early on was the backpaddle. We had heard that the proper whitewater technique is a headlong plunge into the rapids, going in faster than the water so as to gain the leverage needed to twist and turn the boat. After a few tries we learned that it is often just as useful to paddle backward and move slower than the current. In this way it is possible to take advantage of the difference in speed but still have time to pick and choose the route.

Since we had found a whole school of walleyes on Aswapiswan almost a week before, we hadn't had a bite. Now, paddling slowly on a relatively flat section of water, enjoying the sunshine and letting the current do most of the work for us, we decided it was the perfect time to try our luck on the Gods.

The first day on the river, Mike caught the fish we had been waiting for. By that time Steve and I were down to about one and a half fishing poles for the both of us. Even though neither of us had ever broken a fishing rod on a canoe trip, we had decided that it would be smart to bring along some extras just in case something bad happened. It did.

The first time was back on the Winnipeg River, where my backup rod snapped as we tried to escape the dam below. Steve, having given his first extra rod away at the end of Grand Portage, had secured another only to have it catch on a tree during a muddy swamp portage and crack in half. Only hours after that, Steve, fishing with the Fiberglas rod I had picked up at Norway House, had latched onto a northern only to feel the pole shatter in his hands. By this point we were down to just the two ultralight Fenwicks we had carried for the Gods.

But the day before we reached Gods Lake, when we awoke on Touchwood, we were saddened to see that in the darkness we had set the canoe on the tip of Steve's pole and had broken it off. A repair was called for, and we spent several hours with a Swiss Army knife, Shoe Goo and thread before the pole was declared, if not as good as new, at least operational.

That is how we found ourselves on the Gods. Mike and Kub still had all their equipment. But, as we had already put our money into the "biggest fish" pool, we knew we could expect no help from them. Competition is competition.

Mike's fish was a monster by Duluth standards. We had heard so much about the Gods River brook trout that we were becoming dismayed with the swarm of pike that were attacking our lines. Mike's fish brought an end to our disappointment. A full three and a half pounds of dark brown, deep green and bright red, the trout was at least three times bigger than any of us had ever seen taken from the streams at home. It didn't even look like the same species.

We were excited. Pulling our envious eyes from his glistening fish, we caught a glimpse of Mike's lure. With great stealth, we reached into our tackle boxes and eased out the Mepps spinners. This was of course going against our normal lure selection process, wherein we would lay our hands on the box, align ourselves with the fish spirits and try to get the right feel for the day.

On the Gods, everything felt right. That night we pulled the canoes alongside a pool in the middle of about a half mile of rapids—myriad cascading falls and shoots divided by innumerable islands and rock formations. These rapids were not just beautiful; they looked to offer the perfect hiding places for the sought-after trout. A blood oath of secrecy prevents further disclosure.

When I woke up the next morning Steve was already fishing. Just before we had turned in the night before, he had landed his first brookie by casting off the point of our camp. He had pulled it out of the swirls and the rest of us had jumped off the three-foot ledge to land it for him.

Apparently that three-pounder, its red sides gleaming in the glow of the moon, was contagious. Steve had brook trout fever.

There is no known cure for the disease. The only thing that can be done is to make the suffering person as comfortable as possible and let the angler fish for as long as the attack lasts. Given the right spot and enough trout in the waters, the patient can be ready for travel the next day, though the sight of small pools of water can bring on a relapse at any time.

Steve had the fever particularly bad. What was worse, he gave it to the rest of us. By the end of that day we had each hauled up a good 40 brook trout on our barbless hooks. Each of us had a lure to swear by. These brook trout didn't even care.

As usual, the cheaper the lure, the better. I favored a cheap, ugly yellow spoon with red polka dots.

Outdoors writer Sam Cook had told us about the spoons. Loyally following every piece of fishing advice that Sam had ever uttered, we had picked up a dozen.

Up here in the bush we found that some of the spoons were so effective that people would probably have paid almost any price to get ahold of them.

Sometime late in the morning I set off to the other side of the river to a secret spot I had seen the day before. I figured that probably nobody had ever fished that spot since before people had set foot on earth and that a brook trout had been growing there since the end of the last ice age—the lone brook trout of the apocalypse.

Because I knew that such a spot would be hard to reach, I donned the professional brook trout fishing wardrobe. With my shirt tied tightly around my head, I pulled my ever wet boots onto my feet. Into my shirt I stuck the hooks of two of my favorite ugly spoons and in my right hand I carried my rod. Thus equipped, I hopped into the cold water and worked my way through the current.

Half an hour later I found myself standing on a boulder in the middle of the stream, trying to sort out the bird's nest of line coming out of my reel. Somehow the four-pound test line had wound itself around the drag knob and had become irreversibly snarled. Trying to balance myself on the pointed boulder, with one hand I swatted the mosquitoes bearing down on my exposed body while with the other I removed the drag knob. With the concentration and dexterity developed after months in the woods, I ignored the swarming bugs for several crucial seconds and removed the problem-causing knob. Just then I was stung on the back side of my leg. Reflexively, I killed the bug, lost my balance and dropped reel, rod, drag knob and myself into the churning water.

Upon recovery, I realized that somewhere in the depths of Gods River was the little piece of my reel, at one time held in place by my drag knob, that made the reel's drag feature possible. Mentally composing the letter I intended to send to the reel company, I screwed the knob back on and retrieved my line. The contraption worked, but with no drag a heavy pull by a fish could easily break the light line.

Working my way up and around a smaller set of pools, I thought I would try my luck anyway. Seconds after each cast I saw an explosion of red and felt the tug on my line. By carefully playing the line out backward I was able to take advantage of my firm position and managed to land six fish, all from two to three pounds.

After I released them I walked along the shore, coming finally to the bay opposite our camp. Knowing that Steve had had good luck there before, I threw in my own line. On the first cast I pulled in a three-pound trout. On the second, a three and a half. On the third, the line stopped abruptly. "Snagged," I thought.

Not wanting to part with the cheap spoon, I waded into the water to get a better angle on the rock into which I assumed the lure had fallen. But, misjudging both the depth of the bay and the traction I could maintain on the rocks below, I slipped headlong into the icy water. Though surprised, I still had the pole in my hand and began to swim toward the snag. So I could keep the lure's location in sight, I kept the line taut.

Suddenly the line jerked. Then, with a splash, I saw in front of me the jaws of the largest northern I had ever seen. It had my spoon in its mouth and was headed my way! I don't know if it was the splashing of the fish or my screams of terror, but Kub and Steve came running from their fishing places on the river to see what all the excitement was about.

There I was, treading water with both booted feet and one hand while at the same time trying to land a humungous northern on an ultralight trout rod with four-pound line and no drag. I might have been able to do it, too, if I had had both hands free to give out more line. But I was too busy trying to keep my head above water. Tiring of our game, the fish gave one powerful jerk, snapped the line and returned to the depths.

Around the steaked brook trout and garlic bannock that night we discussed the triumphs of the day. The others had fared even better than I. On the far side of the river each had pulled in at least a couple of dozen fish. Steve had found his dream fish, a five and a half pound brookie. That fish qualified him for a spot on the Manitoba Master Angler list for the year. More important, perhaps, the fish assured him of victory in our own fishing contest.

One night on the river we camped at an island literally covered with blueberries. We had made it to the spot in the middle of a long rapids just before dark and decided that it would be best to wait until we could see better before continuing. We made the occasion a food fest. In one pot we poured all the remaining seasonings we had. These included the likes of taco, chili, pork and chicken flavorings. Once this had been cooked into a gooey mess we poured it onto a combination of pasta, rice and mashed potatoes. We couldn't even bring ourselves to name it.

To top off the meal, however, we downed jelly bannock and blueberry cream pie. For the pie we used the trusted graham cracker bannock crust. But because we didn't have any graham crackers we were forced to use just pure brown sugar. As I have said before, it is important to be flexible in the bush.

The next day the skies turned cold and gray and a steady rain began to fall. With our minimal rain protection, the cold crept its way into our bodies and our muscles stiffened. We thought back to Sevareid and Port. We were coming through almost a month earlier than they had, but even our nights were turning crisp, and the evening sky had the smell of autumn.

Sevareid and Port, cold and exhausted, had actually come to blows here on the river. Months traveling with one person alone in the woods can do that. After awhile, having faced days of endless hardship and disappointment, it doesn't take much to set you off.

But for us the river was a friend. Our trials had come earlier, I guess. The big lakes, the waiting, Grand Portage. By the time we got to Gods River we had already been tested, and had toughened and endured, and that made the river all the more rewarding. Of course, things might have been different had we, like those who had come more than 50 years before, awakened each morning to frost and freezing rain.

# CHAPTER NINETEEN

# The Last B.D.

*Now is the winter of our discontent*
*Made glorious summer by this sun of York;*
*And all the clouds that lour'd upon our house*
*In the deep bosom of the ocean buried.*
*Now are our brows bound with victorious wreaths;*
*Our bruised arms hung up for monuments;*
*Our stern alarums chang'd to merry meetings,*
*Our dreadful marches to delightful measures.*

**Wm. Shakespeare**

By the time we got to Red Sucker Rapids we had become pretty good on the river.

Unless the section was marked "falls" on the map, we never stopped the boats. Such spots as "lost-a-man" rapids were notable exceptions.

One particular spot that will stand out in our minds for awhile was the Muskeg Falls. Earlier in the day we had passed around Sturgeon Falls in a light cold mist. When we pulled up to the Muskeg, we were in no mood for another portage.

The section of the river we could see didn't look bad at all. Below us the river split into two sections. The westernmost carried most of the water and looked fierce. To its right, however, was a much smaller flow protected by a long rock island. If we could push over

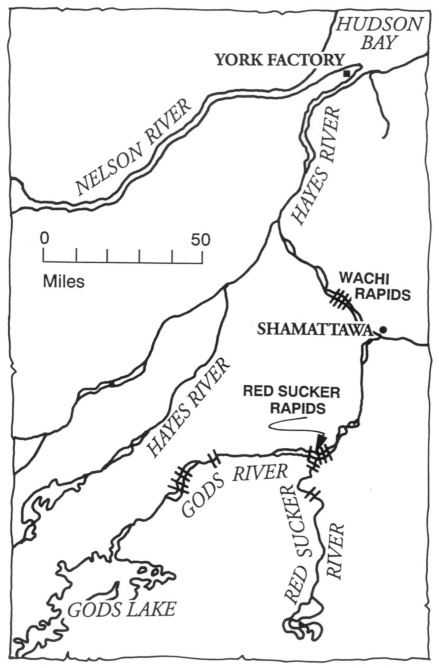

*From the top the rapids looked OK. From the bottom—sure death.*

to that part, it looked like we could make it. There were two complications: the rows of standing waves at the bottom and whatever lay around the bend. Steve and I agonized over the decision while the others pulled into shore. Casting our votes, we decided at last to try to find a portage path. We could at least move some of the gear across and then get a better look from the bottom.

Striking out into the woods, we quickly learned why this was called the Muskeg Portage. Once we had cleared our way through a few yards of rain-drenched undergrowth, we came to an immense muskeg swamp. Picking up what appeared to be a trail we set off, our boots springing up and down in the sloppy humus.

After 10 minutes of this it was apparent that our path was not a portage at all, but one of many animal trails crisscrossing the muskeg. It was a maze, and we were caught in it. Having no real sense of where we were, we pulled out the compass and changed course continually, trying to find the right direction. Left. Now right. Left again.

Perhaps an hour later the paths seemed to converge. After several minutes we appeared at the edge of a steep bank. The water! Carefully, we slid with the gear down to the water's edge and peered around the corner to see if we could make it with the boats. What we saw made our hearts stop. What from the top had looked like a difficult but passable rapids would have meant death for us all. What we saw, hidden from the top by the bend in the river, was the bottom of a gigantic falls.

At Red Sucker Rapids, Sevareid had rolled up their aerial maps and had placed them, covered, on a stick to be picked up later by the trapper who owned the maps.

Here the river was the widest we had seen it. The banks were tall—a good 50 feet—and seemed to be losing their long battle with the river. High above the water at the top of the banks, the spruce looked like a room full of hat stands.

Just before we reached the rapids we saw a strange thing. Ahead on the left side of the canoes we saw movement on the bank. Paddling closer, we saw a whole flock of geese waddling along single file—up the steep cliff! What had ever possessed the birds to take to the ground rather than the air was beyond us.

Wanting to wait out the night before pushing off, we made our own camp on a group of small flat rocks where the Red Sucker flows into the Gods. Each rock was a "room" of its own. We cooked on the kitchen rock, changed on the changing rock and then jumped over the cascading water to the sleeping rock. We even had a guest rock—but no guests.

That night we slept under the stars. We were lulled to sleep by the roar of the waters and woke up in sleeping bags soaked from the spray of the river.

From that wonderful site our camping spots got progressively worse. After the Red Sucker we continued at a good pace. About midday we spotted an object on the clay shore of the river. Swinging the canoe to investigate, we saw the carcass of a sizable bull moose, its flesh all but stripped away. In the hardened mud were the unmistakable prints of large wolves.

Later Mike and Kub saw a phenomenon not often encountered in the North. Paddling swiftly along the smooth water, they heard a slight whoosh behind them. Quickly, they turned. Rising close behind them was a 30-foot swirl of water. A waterspout. In seconds, it was gone.

At that time Steve and I, a few miles farther down the river, heard the whine of an outboard motor. Expecting it to be right behind us, we turned but saw nothing. Twenty minutes later the boat came into view. Equipped with a 10-horse outboard but loaded with six people and stocked with gear, the boat struggled to overtake us. It was a proud moment.

As the sun dipped, we felt that terrible feeling, too many times experienced, of not having a decent spot to spend the night. All summer we had run up against it. Trying to make as many miles a day as possible, we had often passed nice camping spots along the shores to squeeze out another few miles before darkness.

The campsites in the parks of Minnesota were always marked with a red dot on the map. There the only worry was that another group might be occupying the spot.

Here the problem was always whether another spot existed at all. Sometimes good spots were everywhere: either old sites or natural clearings or flat rocks. Other times a thick brush-covered shore would extend for miles.

Usually the extra miles of calm evening paddling made up for the anxiety of not having a home. Other times it did not.

With only an hour or so of light left we found ourselves running the last of the many rapids marked *pishew* on the map. They were long, flat and shallow. At Norway House we had been told they were the "rapids of the lynx." Not that that explained anything.

On either side of us were sloping gravel and mud banks, lower than at the Red Sucker but lined by dense underbrush.

Several miles ahead lay Shamattawa, the settlement where the Shamattawa River (meaning "fast water") flows into the Gods. We wanted to stop there the next morning, so we couldn't pass it that night and had to make camp somewhere above the village.

Gliding smoothly in the strong current we followed the river along as it swung to the south. While passing two small islands we looked half a mile down into the twilight and were astonished to see lights in the worn wooden shacks of a settlement. Shamattawa. There was no choice. We would have to paddle back up the river to a flat-topped spot we had seen a few hundred yards upstream.

We turned the canoes back into the current. "So that's why the Hudson Bay Company people hadn't rowed the York Boats up the Gods." Although smooth, the water was so swift that we had to pull continuously to make any headway at all. A moment's rest and we lost precious ground.

That night we camped in the rain atop a cut-over, mosquito-infested island. When we woke, conditions were not much better. But at least we could leave. Packing up the wet gear, we launched the canoes and paddled the 15 minutes to Shamattawa. When Sevareid and Port had made it to the settlement they had been on the verge of collapse. Chilled to the bone, running out of food and not quite sure where they were, they had found new life in the settlement.

Since Sevareid and Port's coming, Shamattawa had grown—at the expense of York Factory. In the years during the Second World War, we were told, the entire settlement at York Factory had been moved inland to Shamattawa for military reasons.

We could sense the poverty as soon as we pulled the boats up under the Hudson Bay Company flag. Up the steep bank from us was the small company store, surrounded by clusters of rundown one-room plywood houses. When we made it to the top of the bank we were greeted by a group of several men. Gerry Does, a teacher at the high school, invited us over to the community center for a cup of coffee.

Looking much like any American small-town community center, the Shamattawa club was complete with sound system, canteen window and Ping-Pong tables. A young Indian boy walked up and handed Steve a paddle. "Play ya one," he challenged. Steve stood, removed his rain jacket and took the paddle. Minutes later it was Mike's turn. Within an hour we had all fallen, victims of more skillful opponents.

Steve mustered a defense. We hadn't prepared ourselves mentally. How could we have known. "Besides, Ping-Pong's not our sport. Now if you had volleyball . . . ."

While several of the boys tightened the volleyball net, Gerry Does took us over to the radio station. He said we should make an inquiry over the air about moccasins. The Cree make some of the finest moccasins anywhere and sometimes sell their extras. The moccasins are more than just footwear. They are smoke-tanned over low wood fires. The moose or caribou moccasins carry the smell of the North—its very essence. Whether tucked away in a drawer or worn every day, the moccasins can transport you back to the wooded country with just a single magical whiff.

When we got to the radio station we found a few teen-agers running the place. On the turntable spun *The Best of Hank Williams Jr., vol. II.* With a screech, Gerry yanked off the needle, picked up the mike, blew into it several times and announced our arrival. They weren't sure of the range of the broadcast. They thought maybe a mile. Even less certain was the number of radios within that range.

After Gerry reported our interest in moccasins, he felt an urge to interview us live about the trip—a chance at fame! Recovering from our surprise, we collected ourselves and recounted some truly hair-raising adventure stories. We only wished that they had happened to us.

Back at the volleyball court, alone in front of one of the houses, in the middle of the Canadian subarctic tundra, hundreds of miles from the nearest road, sat a full set of Gibson drums. Playing them, ignoring any rhyme or reason in his rhythm, was a small Indian boy, intent on making his mark. If meant as a distraction, it worked.

I'm not trying to make excuses. Sure, it's not at all easy playing volleyball in wet leather boots. Our backs were stiff from the rocks, and our legs were weak from sitting. And spending the night before in a wet sleeping bag didn't do much for preparation, either. But I'm not trying to make excuses. They had some pretty good players.

In fact I think we might have won if Wayne the Mountie hadn't come by and asked if one of us wanted to go on rounds with him. That way we could look for moccasins. I said I'd go and jumped onto the back of his four-wheeler, leaving the others to face our opponents short-handed.

How different it was to be traveling with this northern law officer than it had been with Pastor Crate or Chief Ross at Norway House. At each house here the door was opened just enough for us to get a glance inside. The houses and the receptions were cool.

Shamattawa was a remote-duty post for the Mounted Police. Each Mountie, we learned, is required to serve at such a post for at least two years. Recently, Wayne said, the policy had changed so that no group would stay at one post for an entire two-year tour. "That way we won't have to worry so much about personal attachment to the people," Wayne remarked. "Enforcement will be easier."

But seldom is any change completely positive, and the Mountie knew it. Close connection with a community's problems and character would be lost as well. Wayne would be flown out to Gillam soon and a new team would be brought in.

The children at Shamattawa were curious about us. Learning that we were Americans, they asked if we had any guns. "Are those things bombs?" they asked, pointing at our silver white-gas tanks. At first this puzzled us. But after seeing the movies available for VCR rental in the store, we understood. A strange export, video culture.

One of the children found a woman who was willing to sell some moccasins. With the child interpreting, we sat on the steps of the Hudson Bay Company store and discussed the price. We bought all five pairs the woman offered. She took the fistful of cash, climbed the wooden steps and disappeared into the building.

The store itself was a depiction of life in the North. As we had progressed farther into the wilds, the prices had gone up and selection down. At Shamattawa milk went for five dollars for a half gallon. Other perishable items were equally expensive. Oddly, in addition to the necessary stockpiles of parkas, boots and rifles that lined the dimly lit shelves of the building, there were high-priced luxury goods. It seemed strange, for instance, what with the incredible cost of transportation, that the company had decided to stock the cereal section with Kellogg Variety Packs, each box conveniently making its own bowl.

In the past the Hudson Bay Company had refused to trade in cheap trinkets. Instead, it had offered useful items such as knives, axes and blankets. Looking at the array of cheap plastic toys brought in hundreds of miles through the wilderness, we wondered when this had changed.

Our bargains struck and our sporting pride shattered, we took leave of the village and pushed the canoes out into the current. Our new friends stood silhouetted against the graying sky.

Shamattawa was about 100 miles from York Factory. Although it was late in the afternoon and drizzling when we pushed off, we decided that we would paddle as far as possible. The next day we would push to the end.

Our goal that night was the Wachi Rapids. Known to be among the worst rapids on the river, its two-mile length would best be run with plenty of light. Even paddling as hard as we could, however, we did not reach the fast water until the day was almost gone. Caught up in both the current and our enthusiasm, we pushed straight into the rapids.

Leading, Steve and I maneuvered the boat toward the left of the river. Years before, Sevareid and Port had mistakenly run the rapids on the right on the advice of a trapper. We weren't going to make the same mistake, although from where we sat the whole river looked equally dangerous.

High on the bank we saw the broken hull of an aluminum canoe, then another—grim warnings. Now rushing ourselves headlong into the tumult, we found it nearly impossible to pick a course through the entire length, particularly in the growing darkness.

Actually, the word "rapids" does not accurately describe the Wachi. More appropriate would be some name denoting a continuous series of two-foot waterfalls. Due to the low water of the year we found ourselves grinding off these small ledges, one after another, never unscathed. As the bow descended into the pool ahead, the stern, picking up momentum from the fall, would crash onto the rock bottom. Each time the resulting blow sent shudders through the boat.

By the time we reached the bottom darkness had overtaken us, and Mike and Kub were nowhere to be seen. Assuming that they had holed up just behind us, we paddled another mile or so and landed on a small spit of gravel. Thus began the night of the pathetic.

If it hadn't rained, or if we had put up the tent, things would have been a lot better. But it did, and we didn't, and so it went.

We figured that we were about 80 miles from York Factory. On a lake, this would have been an impossible distance for us to cover in a single day. But, with the help of the current, we thought we just might be able to make it. It would be a biscuit day.

In preparation, we whipped up a good 40 cornbread bannock biscuits. We cooked them over a tiny fire. On the stove we put together a whopping pot of macaroni and cheese. Excited because we no longer had to conserve the powdered cheese, we dumped the remainder of the jar into the pot and waited.

Altogether, we assembled about three pounds of pasta. With the cheese and biscuits, this totaled somewhere around 10,000 calories for the two of us. This meant that we could each expend around 125 calories per mile. We hoped that would do it. Now all we needed was the sun.

To get the earliest possible start we had left the canoe loaded, pulled just out of the water and tied to a bush. We did not undress for the night. In fact, we updressed, and by the time the biscuits were finished we had on every piece of clothing we owned, trying desperately to fend off the oncoming cold.

When the rain started we were already too tired and cold to do much about it. The tent was out of the question. If we pulled that out we would have to pack up a wet tent in the morning. And besides, it must almost be morning.

Steve took drastic measures. Reaching into the clothes pack he pulled out his already soiled sleeping bag, unzipped it and pulled it over his shivering body—muddy boots and all. Then, grabbing the semi-waterproof canoe cover, he rolled up in a nylon ball. We did not talk. That would have meant acknowledging the reality of the situation.

I was even worse off than Steve. I had grabbed our small plastic tarp and wrapped it around me as I lay half in the gravel and half in the bushes. When I stirred after occasional fitful dozes, my wet body was so cold that it ached through and through. Later in the night I reached over to our stove, lit it and huddled over its warmth, the tarp draped over my head. Looking occasionally out at the rain pouring off of Steve's cocoon, I remember thinking that the scene would either make a good advertisement for Coleman or a picture in a Boy Scout manual. It would be titled "how not to camp."

No two people have ever been so happy to see the dawn. The new day couldn't have been more than 10 seconds old—a mere glimmer on the northeastern horizon—before we were on the water, trying to coax our frozen hands to hold the paddles.

Just before we reached the joining flow of the Hayes the sky, which until that point had clung overcast and gloomy, opened up and let through a tremendous burst of sunshine. Somehow this made up for the 40 rain-soaked biscuits in the bag beneath my seat.

On and on we paddled that day. We were determined not to stop until we reached the ocean. The miles slid by. At each turn we looked hopefully around the bend. Each time we expected to see the wide expanse of the great Hudson Bay.

We were tired. We paddled without speaking, knowing that this was the end, but not knowing what to make of it.

When we had left Duluth we had not thought about the end. We hadn't allowed ourselves to. It was too far away, too many miles, too many days.

Even after Lake Superior we still hadn't thought about the end. We had simply moved, struggling through the bad times, loving the good.

Now we didn't want to think of the end. Mostly because that is what it was—the end. The final page of a life we had come to know, and the renewal of a life we had all but forgotten. How would that feel? We had seen the seasons change, and the land.

Late in the afternoon we saw a reminder that this was a different land. First we saw just the movement. Then, pulling closer to the shore, we saw the great majestic frame of a caribou bull. Bigger than any animal we had ever seen, the creature could move with the wind. Catching our scent, it lifted its head, turned and was gone.

Several hours later the river widened. There was a fullness in the wind, a great immensity in the world around us. Looking straight ahead, I stared at the sight I had looked at for three months. The length of the canoe, the faded and disheveled packs and the movement of arms as Steve pulled his paddle through the water.

But now it was not a swamp, a river or a lake that provided the backdrop. It was the ocean. The end. Each drop of water that had hit us, each wild rapid, each bead of sweat from our arms had been headed for this place. The resting place of the rivers.

To signal our arrival clouds gathered overhead into the darkened ball of a powerful storm. We donned our jackets and quickened our blades. Plying our paddles furiously, we pointed the canoe toward the salt water.

Then, rising from the northern shore, high above the steep embankment, beautiful in their contrast with the blackened skies, were the bright colors of the Hudson Bay Company flag.

York Factory.

# CHAPTER TWENTY

# Distant Fires

*Life is the pursuit,
not the capture.*

**Scott Anderson**

Once York Factory was one of the most important buildings in North America.

Nations had fought over its possession, and the people who controlled it controlled a nation—and much of the world. Today much of Canada itself remains a legacy to those adventurers who had dared to call the North their home.

The night we arrived we had little opportunity to reflect on these thoughts. We were more keenly interested in seeking shelter.

After landing the canoe, we scrambled up the steep bank and caught our first clear sight of York Factory, several hundred yards away. The majestic white building stood stolidly against the storm on its lawn of bright green grass.

The heavy rain forced us to paddle away from York Factory itself toward the small weather-worn cabin of the Canadian Park Service, which stood perhaps 200 yards upriver from the Factory.

As we approached we could see that one wall of the cabin was filled with a row of small windows. The windows were covered by an aluminum ladder, which was held in place by ropes. Peering out

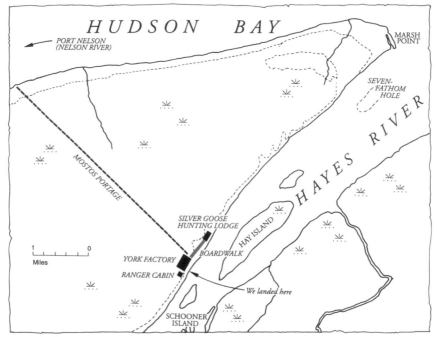

*Distant Fires glow brightest in the heart.*

from under the ladder was the cheerful face of Betty Yeary, the part-time ranger who took time off from winter trapping to watch over the fort.

"Hey," she called, "we weren't expecting you guys for another week. Better come in here and get out of the rain."

We scuttled through the solid door and set down our wet gear.

Over coffee Betty and her partner Jimmy Selter explained that Jim Hatley had told them about us.

We had radioed the Hatleys from Norway House to find out if we could get a boat ride up the Nelson River from York Factory to Gillam. Although we hadn't known it then, Jim Hatley ran the small Silver Goose Lodge just a mile from York Factory.

"With only the five of us up here," Betty said, "it doesn't take long for word to get around. Anyway, you guys better get over to Hatley's now before it gets too dark."

We explained that we had been sleeping out for three months and that another night in the rain wouldn't hurt us.

Jimmy just smiled. "It ain't the rain, it's the polar bears. What d'ya think that ladder there was for?"

We were startled. The ladder across the windows made the cabin a fortress?

"Hey, it's already worked once," said Betty. "But it's not supposed to keep 'em out," she continued, motioning to a dark rifle standing against the table, "it just gives you a little warning."

We slept easy that night in the Silver Goose's small guest cabin. Before blowing out the candles that lit our cool room, we inspected the walls holding out the wind. "It isn't much," said Steve, "but it's better than nylon."

Our macaroni and cheese diet had sustained us well enough so that we each gained 10 pounds over the summer. But let us acknowledge that the hash browns, toast and canned strawberry jam from the kitchen the next morning were a welcome change. During this breakfast Betty arrived and told us that our friends had arrived down at the Factory.

We gulped down our coffee and rushed along the mile-long boardwalk that connected the Silver Goose to York Factory. Betty came along, toting the 12-gauge pump shotgun that never left her side. The first shell was buckshot; the others were slugs. We had our cameras. At least the world would know what had happened.

As we emerged from the tree-lined path we caught our first daytime look at the two-story building. It was magnificent.

Peering into the windows, like two kids at a candy shop, were Mike and Kub.

After a warm reunion on the dewy grass, we talked over our plans. We needed a way home. The night before John Hatley had told us that he no longer ran his boats up the river. We had two alternatives.

The first was to haul our gear five miles across the point and paddle 80 miles up the Nelson River to the train at Gillam. Paddling around the point in the open ocean was too dangerous.

The Nelson route was the way Sevareid and Port had traveled. It had taken them six days to get up the river, and they had found help from some people at York Factory. We had neither the help nor the motors. Our other choice was to fly the distance. It would cost an arm and a leg, but the Nelson route might take a week or more. So we asked Jimmy to let us use his radio phone to call up the bush pilot in Gillam. I related our situation and the pilot said it wouldn't be a problem.

"What's the weather?" he wanted to know.

Glorying in the bright sunshine of the day I replied, "Really nice!" Silence. Apparently that wouldn't do.

"Put Jimmy on for a minute, will you?"

Jimmy relayed the cloud cover, ceiling and wind conditions. Signing off, he turned to me. "Too windy," he said, "tomorrow, maybe the next day." The wind was holding us again.

This time we didn't mind. We were glad to have the time to look around the Factory. Built after hostilities between French and English fur empires had ended, York Factory (so named because it was the residence of the Factor) was constructed not as a military defense, but as the supply depot for a continent. The building in front of us, the main structure in a cluster of many during the settlement's heyday, was built as a large two-story square. An inner courtyard served two purposes. First, it allowed for the safe drying and sorting of furs—away from the ravenous York Factory dogs. Second, it allowed for an extra row of windows in the factory's many rooms. Because of the immense importance of the wares within, no fire was allowed in the building. If the depot had burned while full of goods, the company might well have been ruined.

Without fire, the depot must have been a cheerless place. It would be enough to be deprived of the light; far worse would be to work in a fireless building during the cold, dark winter.

When iron stoves were proven safe enough for use in the factory, they were allowed to burn during the coldest months. Until that time a tiny building, a safe hundred yards from the depot, had housed the settlement's small library. Its main attraction—a crackling fire.

Even up until 1957, when the depot was closed and turned over to the Canadian government as a national historical site, the Company had kept the temperature in the building low. We were told that the Company's manager believed that the best way to keep up productivity would be to keep the trappers out working rather than to have them huddled around the company stove.

The York Factory name had been used over many years for a multitude of buildings and settlements near the end of the Hayes.

The current York Factory, built from 1788 to 1793, is said to be the oldest building still standing on the Canadian permafrost. Its longevity is no accident.

Tired of collapsed and ruined buildings, the Hudson Bay Company carpenters built the structure specially to withstand the shifting and settling of the frost-hardened ground. Their painstaking efforts could be seen throughout the building—as was the fact that the workers had come entirely from the ranks of ship's carpenters.

On the inside the building looked like a ship's interior. Every nook and cranny was filled. Shelves were everywhere. Hooks, latches and cupboards abounded. Rather than fight the moving foundation, the carpenters had built around it. Each joint was notched and a wedge driven in to hold the joists in place. If the walls wanted to shift, the wedge could be moved.

Most striking were the floors. They were not connected to the walls. Thus free to float on the shifting earth, they did not strain against the wooden structure.

In one of the old ground-floor rooms we saw eerie evidence of what the permafrost could do. The standing depot had been built directly over the site of the old stockade. Over the years the foundation boards of that structure, long buried, had pushed themselves through the floorboards of the existing building. Now sticking two feet above the ground, they were rising at a rate of two or three inches per year.

Rising above the slate roof of the depot was a lookout tower. Climbing the narrow steps, we passed through the upper levels of the building. Here the Company had stored the finer trading goods—the silks, the paper, the tobacco. The lower floors were reserved for furs, rum and steel traps.

Poking our heads up into the tower's small wooden turret, we pulled ourselves through the heavy trapdoor. Carved in the worn wooden boards were names from the past. *Ben Henly, 1912. Robert Jenkins, 1872. Steve Baker, 1987.*

On the ground floor we had seen different carvings. Lines at graduated heights had recorded the growth of a child, probably the child of a Factor.

From the roof we could see far past the river we had traveled. What we saw surprised us. From the water we had assumed that the land through which we traveled was thickly wooded. But from our vantage point we saw that the thick spruce grew only along the water. The trees thinned from the shore, leaving only a light grass covered surface. Small ponds dotted the land, each patch of water similarly surrounded, leaving a strange and pockmarked landscape.

York Factory had been built from this wood. The only additions to the native lumber were the large wall braces. These "L" pieces, in ship-building tradition, were made from a single piece of hard root. The stunted spruce of the North being too small, the braces had been imported.

The following day Jimmy branded our paddles. In the tradition of the Company, he burned the "YF" of the factory deep into the tools that had propelled us to the place.

Carrying our prizes with us, we left the depot and returned down the wooden walk to the lodge. The planes were on their way.

Off into the woods on one side of us we saw the remains of a small stone building. The roof was gone entirely and the walls had fallen in pieces to the ground. It was the powder magazine—an explosion's distance from the depot.

To the other side, almost hidden in the deep and tangled growth, was a rusted ship's winch. Supply ships coming from England to York Factory had laid anchor several miles from the post—at a deep spot called the seven-fathom hole. Smaller boats were then used to shuttle the manufactured goods off the ship and replace them with the bundles of furs.

If any boat failed to leave the bay before the ice came in it was hauled up onto shore with the big machine, saving it from the grip of the ice pack. The deep trench left by the keels could still be seen through the brush.

Next to the site of their labor, the bodies of the adventurers had been laid to rest. From a simple wooden cross to an elaborate stone, the grave markers had been tested by the fierce weather. Some of the plots were encircled elaborately by iron fences. But even a fence can't keep out the woods, and dense vegetation had crept through the fences and clung to the carved stone.

On some of the stones the words were still clear, epitaphs to long forgotten residents. On others the words had long ago been scoured from the face of the rock.

I was reminded of Wordsworth's thoughts:

"We die my friend, nor we alone, but that which each man loved and prized in his peculiar nook of earth dies with him, or is changed, and very soon even of the good is no memorial left."

There were other, smaller graves. Each bore the mark of the same year. "Epidemic," whispered Betty.

The graveyard had been built too close to the river. Over the years the rains had come and the banks had declined. Now, when the skies overhead darken and the Hayes begins to swell, the river makes one last claim.

Standing along the muddy beach, surrounded by our piles of gear, we thought back to those whose lives had ended at this spot. Several of the graves had carried not the date of birth, but the date at which the person had started in the North. The old had passed away, a new life had begun, a new life kindled from the fire of the North.

It seemed as if we had been following those distant fires all summer. Often they had dimmed. Our first day out the fires had sputtered to no more than a spark. But they never went out.

We had seen the fires through our sweat on Grand Portage and through the waves of Lake Winnipeg. They were in the children's eyes at Norway House. Never had they burned brighter than the night we had watched the storm break over Forestry Island from the safety of the old wooden church.

Distant fires are around us everywhere. They do not burn just in the North. But in the lands, in the woods and among the lakes and the streams they are easier to see, easier to follow. Everywhere that dream is held and followed to its end, there the distant fires burn. Some only we can see. Others we share with many.

We thought that we would find our fire at York Factory. For years it had burned there before us, always ahead, always beckoning. But distant fires are never reached. At best, it is possible to stand near their ashes, still warm. Looking up, you can see that the fires have moved on, burning brightly somewhere farther in the distance.

At the end of the Hayes I came as close as I have ever been to the fires. But we didn't catch them. Life is the pursuit, not the capture. The chase was our reward—the silent mornings on bright blue water, the rush of the rapids, the call of the loon. Raising our eyes, we saw the fires in the distance. But they were different fires, on a different shore. A time for new dreams.

Standing in silence on that last cold ocean morning, we could not know where those fires lay. But they were about us. We could feel their warmth. On that day, on that shore, that was enough.

Overhead, a roar of planes. A canoe had carried us from our homes to this distant place. Now it was to be carried, tied to a pontoon of the Beaver floatplane. This had worried us. But Jimmy assured us that the pilots were professionals—they'd done the operation a thousand times and had all the right gear.

When the first pilot landed we greeted him warmly. He looked tired, his eyes red and ringed in darkness. "Right on," he said. "Hey, you guys got any rope for tying those boats on, eh?"

We didn't. We smiled. One of these days we'd get it right. All we needed was another summer.

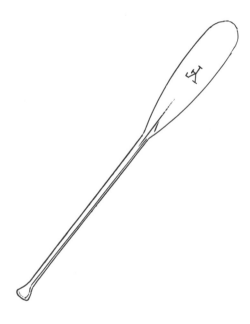

# Bering Bridge: The Soviet-American Expedition from Siberia to Alaska   by Paul Schurke

Twelve Soviet and American adventurers set out from Siberia in mid-winter 1989 on an epic journey across 1,000 miles of arctic tundra. This unprecedented trek was the first expedition since the advent of the Cold War to travel between the USA and the USSR across the Bering Strait.

Visiting native Siberian villages along their route, these dog sled diplomats helped build a bridge of friendship that now connects people of the Bering Strait region, and all citizens of the USA and the USSR.

More than just a dramatic adventure, *Bering Bridge* is a story of peace.

Hardcover, 240 pages, photos
ISBN 0-938586-31-9    $17.95

# Wilderness Daydreams

Escape to the wilderness — no matter where you are! Naturalist Douglas Wood serves as a guide for your personal wilderness journey. Relax and enjoy the sounds and images of nature as Doug's gentle voice leads you to places of solitude, peace and renewal. With original guitar music and environmental sounds.

| Wilderness Daydreams 1: Canoe/Rain | Wilderness Daydreams 2: Island/Spring | Wilderness Daydreams 3: Campfire/Stream |
| --- | --- | --- |
| Side A: Canoe trip with gentle guitar accompaniment. (23 min) Side B: Safe haven in the rain with background sounds of the storm. (23 min) Audio cassette/$9.95 | Side A: Island trek with soothing classical guitar accompaniment. (23 min) Side B: Sunny spring day with authentic sounds of the marsh. (23 min) Audio cassette/$9.95 | Side A: Gaze into the campfire lulled by a quiet guitar. (23 min) Side B: Explore a forest stream with sounds of nature all around. (23 min) Audio cassette/$9.95 |

Hardcover, 192 pages, $16.95
ISBN 0-938586-17-3

# Quiet Magic *by Sam Cook*

The magic is there, right before you, in a hundred little ways.

It's the whisper of line leaving a fishing reel at sunrise in a quiet bay. It's the rattling of a sled dog on its stake-out chain outside the tent on a snowy night. It's the first pungent scent of smoke from the fire.

The magic is waiting for you. Go. Let the wind harden your face. Feel the soul of the North Country. Find the quiet magic.

Now the *Quiet Magic* of the North Country is yours, in this delightful collection of stories and essays by Sam Cook.

Step outside and marvel at the grand experience of the North — the power of a building storm on the greatest of the Great Lakes; the glory of Northern Lights in the shimmering night sky; the embracing, absolute silence of a snowhouse.

Or stay inside with *Quiet Magic* and savor Sam Cook's sensitivity and gentle humor. Look outward to discover the North Country; look inward to discover yourself.

You hold the *Quiet Magic* in your hands. Let it take you away.

*"For those of us inclined to view the outdoors in terms of grand adventures, the word pictures in Sam Cook's latest literary sketch pad are poignant reminders of the depth of wonder and enjoyment that can be drawn from every experience in nature's world."*

Paul Schurke, arctic adventurer

*Sam's stories will strike a responsive chord in anyone who has dipped a paddle into a northern Minnesota lake. One's own memories and dreams of the wilderness will be rekindled upon reading Quiet Magic.*

Craig and Nadine Blacklock

**Quiet Magic winner of the Northeastern Minnesota Book Award 1989**

Hardcover, 192 pages, $14.95
ISBN 0-938586-09-2

# *Up North* by Sam Cook

Up North is a certain way the wind feels on your face and the way an old wool shirt feels on your back. It's the peace that comes over you when you sit down to read one of your old trip journals, or the anticipation that bubbles inside when you start sorting through your tackle box early in the spring.

Each of us has an Up North. It's a time and place far from here and now. It's a map on the wall, a dream in the making, a tugging at one's soul.

In this memorable collection of essays and stories, columnist Sam Cook portrays the enchanting North Country that is as much a state of mind as a geographical area.

*Up North* captures the mystic moods, seasonal subtleties and colorful characters that fill the landscape from the Minnesota canoe country to the vast expanse of the Northwest Territories. These stories are more than mere tales of hunting and fishing, paddling and portaging. They are journeys into the soul. In his witty, touching style, Sam Cook offers insights about life set against the backdrop of the North Country's magic.

Sam Cook trekked north from his native Kansas in 1976 to work for an outfitter in the Superior-Quetico canoe country. Now he uses Duluth, Minnesota, as "base camp" for his warm, insightful outdoors columns for the Duluth News-Tribune.

*"An uncommonly compassionate writer, Cook is arguably Minnesota's best-loved newspaper columnist . . . "*

William Souder, *Minnesota Monthly*

*"Sam can bring memories of a blizzard into your living room with such remembrance that even though you may be sitting in front of a roaring fire you will feel the bite of the snow upon your face. Sam is good!"*

Wally Pease, *The Outdoor Press*, Washington State

# Order Form

 800-247-6789 (USA) TOLL FREE
218-728-6807
218-728-2631 FAX

 Pfeifer Hamilton Publishers
1702 E Jefferson Street
Duluth, MN 55812-2029

> Quantity discounts are available for retail distribution,
> executive gifts and incentive programs.

**SHIP THE FOLLOWING**

| Quantity | Title | Price | Total |
|---|---|---|---|
| _____ | Distant Fires | 12.95 | _____ |
| _____ | Bering Bridge | 17.95 | _____ |
| _____ | Quiet Magic | 16.95 | _____ |
| _____ | Up North | 14.95 | _____ |
| _____ | Wilderness Daydreams 1 | 9.95 | _____ |
| _____ | Wilderness Daydreams 2 | 9.95 | _____ |
| _____ | Wilderness Daydreams 3 | 9.95 | _____ |

Item Total _____

(Minnesota residents add 6% tax)

(Duluth residents add 7% tax) _____

Shipping $3.00

TOTAL AMOUNT ENCLOSED _____

**PAYMENT METHOD**

_____ Check enclosed payable to Pfeifer-Hamilton

Bill my: _____ VISA _____ Master Card

# _____ - _____ - _____ - _____ Expires _____

Signature: _____

Name _____

Address _____

City/State/ZIP _____

Daytime Phone ( _____ ) _____